THE MODERN POET

THE MODERN POET

Essays from *the Review*

Edited by Ian Hamilton

MACDONALD · LONDON

FIRST PUBLISHED IN GREAT BRITAIN IN 1968 BY
MACDONALD & CO. (PUBLISHERS) LTD.
49 POLAND STREET, LONDON W.1

MADE AND PRINTED IN GREAT BRITAIN BY
UNWIN BROTHERS LIMITED
WOKING AND LONDON

CONTENTS

EDITOR'S NOTE

The Modern Poet is a selection of essays from the first fifteen issues of *the Review*, a small magazine of poetry and criticism which I founded in 1962. Apart from one or two very minor emendations, the essays appear here as originally published. I have also included three 'conversations'—the now celebrated dispute between A. Alvarez and Donald Davie and interviews with William Empson and Robert Lowell—and a few poems.

A publication like *the Review* needs friends almost as much as it needs enemies, and I could fill a page with messages of gratitude to all those who have helped the magazine in one way or another. The chief debt, though, is to its contributors who, unpaid and uncomplaining, have turned in work which, in my view, ranks with the best poetry criticism of the last decade.

IAN HAMILTON

COLIN FALCK

DREAMS AND RESPONSIBILITIES

A. Alvarez offers *The New Poetry** as what "really matters" from the last decade and not as a complete guide to the English scene today. Our trouble, he thinks, is that the poetic upheaval which began with the experimental techniques of Eliot and Pound was prevented from coming to anything in this country by a series of "negative feed-backs". First we had the reversion to traditional forms in chic modern guise by Auden in the Thirties, then the high rhetoric and anti-intellectualism of the Forties, and finally the wry flatness of the Fifties Movement. In various ways these all helped to stem the revolution and re-foster our English beliefs in the essential order, politeness and controllability of life. And the result is that "the concept of gentility still reigns supreme" in our poetry. But this genteel stance gets more and more difficult to maintain in an age of mass evil and depth psychology, and the poets who matter now are those who can experience the real underlying disintegration and confront it with the necessary formal skill and intelligence. Those marshalled in this book include two Americans, Berryman and Lowell, and a selection of more recent British names.

We should salute Alvarez for his seriousness, but I don't think his Introduction really comes over as the piece of propaganda he wants it to be. It throws up ideas about verse-forms, emotion, evil, gentility and much else, but in the end does very little to distinguish or relate them all. So that when the "new seriousness" is eventually defined as "the poet's ability and willingness to face the full range of his experience with his full intelligence" we don't feel very much the wiser and have almost no cutting edge for the actual choosing of poems. The anthology itself is in fact far less partisan and more representative than its Introduction pretends: there are no wild inclusions, and if the decade's best poems are mostly here we are still left to our own criteria for picking them out from the rest. Sometimes the chosen poems even seem to conflict with the vague criteria we are given, but there is no attempt

* *The New Poetry*. Selected and introduced by A. Alvarez. Penguin, 1962.

to explore this or to ask what it shows. How, we want to know, does formal control of a poem relate to psychological control of what it's about?—because with his talk about traditional forms and the concept of gentility Alvarez seems to see the urgency of a poem's content and the discipline of its finished verse-form as pulling always in opposite directions. In what sense can traditional forms go out and come back in? Isn't Pound's rhyming as important as whatever is most modern in his technique? Ted Hughes is one of the most favoured poets in this selection, but in what sense does he face the "full range" of his experience? More generally, if England stayed genteel by missing the war and the concentration camps (as Alvarez suggests), how come the Americans are so good? What feelings do John Berryman's diffusely intellectual verses really bring us to the "quick" of? The questions multiply, and it would be silly to think they could all be met in a short introduction (or here). But the danger, if they are not even allowed to arise, is that we shall find ourselves driven back into the personal and irrational attitudes that the "new seriousness" was meant to save us from, while the "new seriousness" itself remains circular and unpersuasive: "I am serious—good poetry is convincing—try this."

Alvarez writes that

> The final justification of experimentalism lay, of course, beyond mere technique. The great moderns experimented not just to make it new formally, but to open poetry up to new areas of experience. The kind of insights which had already been substantiated by the novelists—by Melville, Dostoyevsky, Lawrence, and even, at times, by Hardy himself— seemed about due to appear in poetry. The negative feed-backs came into action to stop this happening.

Now it isn't clear from this exactly what these novelists' insights were, but whatever the answer there is something wrong somewhere. Are we talking about England or the whole world? If the world, it's obviously misleading to treat Eliot and Pound as a beginning: they were more like the first breakthrough into English (except Poe) of a tradition which came at least from Baudelaire, and which also bred surrealism and the high experimentalism of the American Twenties. This tradition is far from easy to characterise, but what it represented in one of its aspects was some kind of cumulative failure of confidence in language and meaning as a whole: from this point of view it is part

of the general tendency of the past century and a half which is sometimes called existentialism. The same thing has haunted the European
novel since Dostoyevsky, but it came earlier in poetry, not later; so
that to talk of the novelists' insights appearing later in poetry is, if I am
right about what these insights essentially were, rather misleading.
Eliot, I suggest, experienced a good deal of the existentialist crisis
within his poetry, and we run the risk of misrepresenting and even
underrating him if we try to concentrate on his techniques and look
for our specifically modern content elsewhere. Eliot's "raid on the
inarticulate / With shabby equipment always deteriorating" and
"intolerable wrestle / With words and meanings" are not just over-
civilised temporisings: they mark a real uncertainty about the possibility
of saying anything at all, just as his earlier "I should have been a pair
of ragged claws / Scuttling across the floors of silent seas" recalls
nothing so much as the sick and lawless world of Sartre's La Nausée. It
may be that we reject Eliot's own religious solution. In a way this is
another matter; but there is a sense too in which it is just the point.
This is because the crisis of language and meaning which has beset
modern literature is very much a crisis of belief: it is a late result of our
loss of the common world of ideas and values which was once
guaranteed by religion. In this respect we are on the last arc of a
trajectory which began with the Middle Ages. It is possible, obviously,
to exaggerate the uniqueness of this phase: the greatest poetry has
always called the entire world in question and has always worried
about the difficulty of saying what we mean. But it is only recently
that this worry has become highly explicit and all-pervasive and any
poetry whatever has seemed to lie under some kind of metaphysical
threat. At the extreme of this awareness the whole ordinary referential
power of words has seemed to be threatened: they "slip, slide, perish, /
Decay with imprecision", and language takes on a kind of opacity in
its own right instead of being a clean instrument for dealing with the
world. Again, some such opacity is the necessary condition of all poetry,
and is in fact the element in which it works: R. P. Blackmur has
spoken of poetry as "reasoning the unknown of which we are possessed
into the known". But in the modern situation this opacity has sometimes
seemed dangerously total, the "known" of which we are possessed
dangerously fluid and uncertain. Categories loosen and interweave,

and subjectivity and objectivity become harder to disentangle. This kind of derangement dominates the work of a poet like Rimbaud, and Rimbaud's solution was to surrender to the disorder deliberately and systematically. Mallarmé, on the other hand, tried to purge language of its practical meaning altogether and make his poetry a pure structure with no reference beyond itself. When we trace this conflict to Eliot we find a different kind of tactic at work. In Eliot's poetry the sharpest and most concrete perceptions are beautifully realised, only to be dissolved again in the meditations of the ever-present "I" that controls the poem from within: his abstract doubt holds concrete experience in a continual cat-and-mouse relationship, and this play of belief and disbelief is resolved in the end only through Christian symbolism. Pound shows very much the same kind of awareness in "Mauberley". And other reactions to the crisis produced the purer subjectivity of Imagism and Dada and, more profoundly and maturely, the strange synaesthetic poetry of Hart Crane. Wallace Stevens faced these same problems in a rather explicitly philosophical way.

So it is certainly true that Eliot and Pound opened up English poetry to new experience. But their forms were modern precisely because the experience they so perfectly articulated was the modern experience itself. The crisis of meaning which Eliot faced is so much a part of our ordinary sensibility now, and to such a degree pervades or even constitutes the "quick" of our feelings, that the poet who denies or ignores it courts irrelevance and ephemerality. The loss of innocence is radical and there is no quick and simple redemption: at this moment in our history we can't decide to go back and write like Yeats.* All right, it may be said, but is this all? What has it to do with gentility and with England? Weren't Dostoyevsky and Lawrence concerned with violence and evil, not just with words? These are hard questions; but they are not quite to the point either, I think. Part of the answer is that these things are not really so distinct. The centre of Dostoyevsky's vision is the *Notes from Underground*, where the crisis of meaning finds its most intense expression; and there is a lot in common between Lawrence and even the most dislocated fantasies of Kafka. The relation between

---

* *I should now want to qualify some of this argument. I think I have over-existentialised Eliot here, and I think Alvarez was right to suggest that there are important insights in modern prose fiction which have not yet been explored in verse.*

meaninglessness and violence can seem very close and direct. "When action involves choosing between worlds, not moving in a world," Iris Murdoch has written, "loving and valuing, which were once the rhythm of our lives, become problems. Emotions, which were the aura of what we treasured, when what we treasured was what we unreflectively did, now glow feverishly like distant *feux follets*, or have the imminent glare of a volcanic threat." This is something we all know about. Modern violence and evil spring from a repressive civilisation which defies our instincts and turns us over to unchannelled emotions. And it is for literature to try and make sense of this by revealing possibilities within us which transcend the existing order: art comes, as Rilke said, "from this tension between contemporary currents and the artist's untimely conception of life", and offers us "the sensuous possibility of new worlds and times". But poetry itself must be concerned with this re-creation of vision and meaning in a very pure way indeed, and not with the conveying of desperation or emotional shock. This is why the earlier questions weren't quite to the point: there is more room for explicit blood and passion in the novel or on the stage than there is in the poem, simply because of the kind of media these are and the kind of order they aim for. They depend—as poetry does not—on character and drama, and there is time to clear up after even the messiest disasters. It is right, then, to condemn the "negative feedbacks" for losing us Eliot's complex modern awareness here in England; but this is not the same as wanting the poet to deal directly with violence. And the too-uncritical championing of Lawrence, Lowell and Hughes (on these grounds) could lead us into as complete a betrayal of English poetry as any of Alvarez's "feed-backs".

This argument has many conclusions, some of which we may find ourselves arriving at quite independently, and I think it is worth listing a few of them for whatever light they throw on the idea of a "new seriousness" and on Alvarez's own interpretation of this idea. One is the weight that now falls on poems coming out of interpersonal experience: this follows directly from the volcanic part that such experience plays in our lives today. As Eliot has said, "When morals cease to be a matter of tradition and orthodoxy ... then personality becomes a thing of alarming importance." Our experience of others is an increasingly vital means by which our awareness grows. Another result is the dominant rôle of shorter poems. This is because in the effort now towards purely poetic re-creation of meaning the long poem risks either simply reflecting the private pattern of the poet's mind, or else eking out with conscious but poetically unsustained thought. The would-be long poem must settle with the *Quartets* and *The Bridge* first.* In the same way, didacticism is out, and with it the kind of shrewd Movement message-poem which is really a lot of unrelating images strung on one long idea. This goes, in fact, for any abstraction and discursiveness which isn't involved essentially in a pattern of direct lyrical re-creation—and therefore includes the maundering most fashionable in America today which harps on, round and through the "language-problem" itself to the point of complete etiolation and beyond. All this follows from the kind of total enterprise that modern poetry distinctively is: Blackmur's characterisation of Eliot's poetry as (in Coleridge's words) "bringing the whole soul of man into activity" applies to serious modern poetry in general. But it follows, to the same degree, that serious poems may now seem less concerned with experience than they used to be and more with experiencing: far less can be taken for granted, and honesty has driven us back to the kind of basic lyrical awareness that we find in our most essential poetry since Eliot. This gives a clue, of course, to today's apparent problem about subject-matter: the difficulty in finding subject-matter is really an honest half-way stage to seeing that it is the idea of subject-matter itself which is now problematic. (Leavis's quotation from Bottrall at the front of *New Bearings in English Poetry* shows this in an almost moving way.) The choice is not between writing "about" things or writing "about" our own private (and, it is often implied, morbid) states of mind: it is the realm between which is the exact domain of poetry. Blake anticipated this when he said "We are led to believe in a lie / When we see with not through the eye". And finally, if poetry means bringing our whole soul into activity, the modern tendency we get from Eliot and Pound towards a poetic diction based in ordinary language and felt speech-rhythms is easy to understand. So is the need to be very intelligent.

There seem to me to be hints here, if no more, towards some better

---

* *I should now argue that some kind of continuity may exist between the long poem and the symbolist novel. What this question really turns on is the essential nature of verse.*

criteria and more principled criticism than we get from Alvarez's mere emphasis on "the poet's ability and willingness to face the full range of his experience with his full intelligence". What we need, obviously, is not to reject this formula, but to give it a cash value in terms of actual poetry. And at the risk of being Procrustean and negative in the space available I shall try and do this with some of the poets in Alvarez's actual selection. I am not so much interested in proving a theory here as in the coherence of the position that Alvarez seems to hold in *The New Poetry*; but the only test of criticism in the end is whether we can give rationality to something we already dimly feel.

John Berryman, the first recommended American in this book, is very intelligent indeed, but his intelligence seems to me to operate to the exclusion of most other serious poetic qualities. Berryman's poems lack a real voice of their own and move with ventriloquial facility through a baffling range of other people's idioms, from wistful Auden ("Spares homosexuals, the crippled, the alone, / Extravagant perception of their failure; / Looks only, cynical, across them all / To the delightful Avenue and its lights") to a kind of assonant headiness based on Hopkins ("Thick night, where the host's thews crack like thongs / A welcome, curving abrupt on cheek & neck"). Whatever the style, the poems mostly lack any real texture of personal and concrete sensibility ("The Song of the Tortured Girl" is almost an exception), with the result that the heavy thinking they all contain ("History is approaching a speechless end, / As Henry Adams said") has no lyrical centre to draw poetic meaning from and so to justify its presence in the poem. Whatever concreteness there is usually stands as illustration to some already explicit theme (the whole of "Ball Poem" is like this), so that each poem as a whole remains awash in unredeemed abstractions and finally offers us no more than its elements contribute separately. A prevailing sentiment in the poems seems to be the sort of edgy nostalgia that comes out most clearly in "The Statue" ("Fountains I hear behind me on the left, / See green, see natural life springing in May / To spend its summer sheltering our lovers, / Those walks so shortly to be over"). But cut off from poetic articulation the feeling remains self-indulgent and often banal, even where it springs from a potentially urgent situation. The different styles it assumes, on the other hand, having no personal voice to inform them, all sound mandarin and unvital, periphrastic studies in a whole repertoire of worn-out poetical fashions. Even in the souped-up diction of "Whether there is Sorrow in the Demons" the most desperate phrases ("Stone-tufted ears", "Only the lost soul jerks") ring strangely dead. I don't understand, then, why Berryman should be offered to us as one of two main examples to follow. At greater length I would certainly argue for the importance and value of "Homage to Mistress Bradstreet" as a whole, but this really has little bearing on Berryman's relevance for mid-twentieth-century England.

Robert Lowell, on the other hand, could well be the most important poet now writing in English, and my remarks here can only be quite marginal to his central merit. The risk in taking Lowell's later poems as an example, as Alvarez implicitly does, is that we may find ourselves being led, in the name of honesty and coping "nakedly" with experience, to sacrifice too much that is essential to poetry itself. Reading Lowell one often feels that an order is being imposed on words and perceptions externally by some kind of discursive or rhetorical control where the experiencing itself failed to reveal order of an internal poetic kind. The danger is that we might come to see this as a virtue and not as an artistic shortcoming. In the late poems Lowell has lines that one would trade in whole other celebrated outputs for ("blossoms on our magnolia ignite / the morning with their murderous five days' white"), but these moments rarely compose into sustained vision, and there is an ever-present tendency for the poems to mirror the chaos of experience without overcoming it. The actual poetic texture is always dangerously thin. In "Man and Wife", which seems to me one of the best of the *Life Studies*, the opening lurid perception (of which the magnolia lines above are a part) fuses with later reflection ("its hackneyed speech, its homicidal eye—") and generates powerful poetry. But often there is a collapse into psychological self-analysis ("I myself am hell, / nobody's here—") which confirms the disorder of the poem without redeeming it, or into a loose trail of observations held together by a kind of piecemeal rhetoric ("These victorious figures of bravado ossified young"). Either way the poems then become rambling and contingent and sometimes seem pregnant with whole new lengths of themselves like some kind of hallucination. What this means, of course, is that Alvarez's "coping with disturbance nakedly and without evasion" is a misleading rubric. The very act of artistic representation precisely is a means of evasion, and this is its point: too naked, we fail to objectify at all and may only confuse or shock. Lowell's later poems are often naked and personal in this bad sense. In the end nakedness can only mean some kind of avoidance of self-deception; but this is part of the definition of art and tells us very little about its proper content.

Lowell, in fact, seems too unable or unwilling to let words create a basis of meaning by themselves, and his poems often feel more hewn out than inspired, as if very little in them ever surprised Lowell himself. And when the wrestle with words and meanings becomes as gladiatorial and unsubmissive as this there is a real threat to the kind of reflection-within-experience which provides the basic strength of poetry, and which governs the unity and self-containment of any single poem and the shape it will most naturally assume. This comes out, I think, in the shape Lowell's poems actually have. In the highly untraditional verse-forms of *Life Studies* it is not the poetic content which dictates the form, as Alvarez seems to suggest, and as it undoubtedly is with, say, Eliot. There is no trace of Eliot's imagistic word-placing, and Lowell's lay-out and line-breaks are often wilfully chopped-up and undramatic ("Thirsting for / the hierarchic privacy / of Queen Victoria's century, / she buys up all / the eyesores facing her shore / and lets them fall"). Instead, the form is determined by superficial rhyming requirements which themselves have no further obvious justification ("Man and Wife", "Skunk Hour", again). In turning against his earlier metrics and diction Lowell followed a sound instinct, but he then seems to have been left with no clear idea of what to do instead and no real way of arresting the general drift towards prose. With so little guidance from the internal shape of his poems there was bound to be something arbitrary-seeming about the formal observances he kept up after the break. (In the earlier poems the Catholic rationale helped to justify the rhetoric and metre, but it remained extrinsic to the poetry: there is really the same weakness of essential poetic organisation in earlier and later alike.) The result, at the extreme, is the kind of tricksy lay-out and rhyming that comes at the end of "To Delmore Schwartz" (not in this book: "In the ebb- / light of morning, we stuck / the duck / -'s web- / foot, like a candle, in a quart of gin we'd killed"), which is formally like the later *Life Studies* only more so. On the other hand, the most striking thing about "Man and Wife", the best organised of these poetically, is the way it almost seems to require three regular stanzas of some kind. (And much the same is true of "Home After Three Months Away", which is also very fine, although incomprehensibly missing from this anthology.) So although Lowell brings up questions of form very acutely he doesn't by any means settle them, and his own later forms, far from being the necessary expression of his content (as Alvarez seems to imply), are more like lip-service paid to formal demands which this content gives him little help in meeting, but which some lingering respect for the traditional apparatus of poetry prevents him from refusing entirely. It may be for this reason that Lowell often seems stronger as a translator than as an original poet: his translations are original poems built on a framework which is to a greater or lesser degree there already.

The most heavily represented English poet in this anthology is Ted Hughes. Alvarez makes clear his admiration for Hughes when, comparing Larkin's "At Grass" with Hughes's "A Dream of Horses", he writes that Hughes's poem is "a serious attempt to re-create and so clarify, unfalsified and in the strongest imaginative terms possible, a powerful complex of emotions and sensations. Unlike Larkin's, Hughes's horses have a violent, impending presence. But through the sharp details which bring them so threateningly to life, they reach back, as in a dream, into a nexus of fear and sensation. Their brute world is part physical, part state of mind." This seems to me very revealing. Do we clarify our emotions merely by re-creating them? I suspect that this idea governs Alvarez's judgement of poetry in a very general way and may explain a great deal about this anthology in particular. Alvarez suggests that Hughes's strength is this ability to re-create and "so" clarify our emotions, whereas it seems to me on the contrary that the real limitation of Hughes's animal poems is precisely that they conjure emotions without bringing us any nearer to understanding them. They borrow their impact from a complex of emotions that they do nothing to define, and in the end tell us nothing about the urban and civilised human world that we read the poems in. If they reach back, "as in a dream", to a nexus of fear and sensation, this is just the point and the reason why they frequently fail as poetry: one difference between dreams and art is that art deepens our understanding while dreams on their own do not. Larkin's horses are more profound than Hughes's, in fact, because they show us something about the relationship between the horses' world and our own instead of just frightening us with theirs.

Hughes's poetic world is really a prehistoric world of natural violence, where humanity has only the barest fingerhold: when the poems are not about animals they are often about inanimate nature ("October Dawn"), and they give no place to emotions and experience of an essentially human kind. In this sense Hughes is a nature poet, a kind of tough mid-century Blunden (compare their pikes or their Octobers), and makes no serious attempt to face the "full range" of his experience: the experience and emotions that control his poems are frequently those that we share with animals, and these are evoked "as in a dream" more often than they are explored. It would be one thing to write a single poem or two out of this idea, but to make it the dominant theme of an entire output is quite another. When Hughes makes a direct attempt on human experience the result is often catastrophic: when people feature in the poems they serve as occasions for the poet's own cocksure imagination ("Famous Poet", "Vampire") or comfortable romanticising ("A Woman Unconscious") and never imply a real human engagement or any of the self-doubt that this might sometimes carry with it. It is always hard for a poet to write about people, because there is a deep and perpetual antagonism between human individuals and the poetic images through which we attempt to understand them. But this is what gives poetry its work and its justification. With Hughes the victory goes simply and completely to the images ("Deep under the city's deepest stone / This grinning sack is bursting with your blood"), and the result is a cruel absence of compassion and a profound denial of the capacity for growth, love and uniqueness which makes human beings human (and not simply one more species of animal). Hughes's poems are often very fine technically, with sharp detail and imagery and a tense motion perfectly suited to their dramatic content ("Pike", "Esther's Tomcat", especially). From this point of view they are perhaps unequalled by the other poets in this anthology (though by Alvarez's account technique ought almost to be one of their weaknesses). But their most important lesson, it seems to me, concerns what can and cannot be done in an idiom which is decreasingly workable and relevant today and which involves, with Hughes at any rate, a lack of any essential commitment to the human world and its conflicts. It seems to me that Alvarez can rate Hughes so extravagantly only on the basis of a misguided, and I suspect ultimately dangerous, view of what poetry is.

Philip Larkin, on the other hand, has produced some of the most genuinely post-Eliot poetry that we have yet had in this country. At his best Larkin comes near to Eliot's kind of seriousness, but in his earlier poems the offhand manner and flat Movement diction usually work against this seriousness in a fatal way: Larkin seems to adopt a wryer version of Eliot's old man persona and to be happy only when he can collapse the intellect into knockabout so as to undermine the poetry entirely and save himself from emotional self-exposure. Many whole poems are variations on some simple self-deprecating theme, like "Toads", which merely develops the lines "For something sufficiently toad-like / Squats in me, too", and "Poetry of Departures", which is a very unpoetic rationalisation of the poet's inability to chuck up everything and clear off. Sometimes the poems just hint coyly at unnamed horror in the manner of Auden's "The Witnesses" ("Going", for example: "There is an evening coming in / Across the fields, one never seen before, / That lights no lamps"). And there are lines, like those at the end of "If My Darling", which read like surly no-nonsense echoes of the *Quartets* ("the incessant recital / Intoned by reality, larded with technical terms, / Each one double-yolked with meaning and meaning's rebuttal: / / For the skirl of that bulletin unpicks the world like a knot, / And to hear how the past is past and the future neuter / Might knock my darling off her unpriceable pivot"), as well as being wilfully ugly and anti-poetic in the usual churlish Movement way. This manner sometimes overflows into more technical things and issues in bad rhyming (grass/cars; is/destinies/seriousness; surprising/wise in), weak line-breaks ("Wide farms went by, short-shadowed cattle and / Canals . . .") and a frequent tendency for material to be pushed around so as to fill out complex forms.

It has also been said that the feeling in Larkin's poems is thin. This is often true, and particularly in the earlier idea-poems where it comes out as a persistent kind of self-pity. Some of the more impersonal poems, on the other hand, are quite different and contain very impressive lines and passages ("At Grass", for instance: this poem is surely as much concerned with human life—with freedom and security, with youth, age and religious faith—as with horses). And when Larkin has the courage to write really honestly and without self-deception the result is often powerful and moving. This happens in parts of "Church Going" (not in this anthology) and in some of the more recent poems. At these times Larkin finds a very individual poetic idiom which brings together Eliot's intellectual tension and reflectiveness, Auden's sharp sense of contemporary things and scenery, and a very direct emotional strength based in ordinary speech and asserting itself firmly beneath the elegance of the finished style. These qualities seem to me to come out well in the lines which conclude the train journey in "The Whitsun Weddings":

> I thought of London spread out in the sun,
> Its postal districts packed like squares of wheat:
> There we were aimed. And as we raced across
>   Bright knots of rail
> Past standing Pullmans, walls of blackened moss
> Came close, and it was nearly done, this frail
> Travelling coincidence; and what it held
> Stood ready to be loosed with all the power
> That being changed can give. We slowed again,
> And as the tightened brakes took hold, there swelled
> A sense of falling, like an arrow-shower
> Sent out of sight, somewhere becoming rain.

Reflection and vision come together here, and there is a lyrical intensity at the very end which resists paraphrase entirely. The poem treats a large theme in genuinely poetic terms and at moments touches the power of those parts of "The Dry Salvages" that it so much recalls. It also has emotional courage and human warmth, and in all these ways seems to me to leave the basic attitudes of the Movement well behind. This is worth saying, if only to counter the idea that the control and discipline of a poet like Larkin (or of any poet) acts as some kind of limitation, even if a necessary one, on the poetic intensity he can achieve today. I suggested that this was wrong in discussing Lowell and Hughes, and I think there is enough real poetry in Larkin to dispose of the idea altogether.

Other poets in this book contribute less crucially to its main design
and I can only mention one or two of them briefly. R. S. Thomas is
among the best, and his poems have a clarity and self-containment
which is uncommon. Sometimes they spread out into prose, and there
are religious intrusions which are given no force in terms of experience
and which short-circuit the poetry unnecessarily. But this is far from
general, and the poems are often very powerful on their own sharp and
concrete level and have a serious human quality. Thom Gunn has been
closely studied in articles by Michael Fried (*New Left Review*, Novem-
ber/December 1961) and John Fuller (*the Review*, April/May 1962,
see p. 17) and many of their conclusions fit in with my argument here.
Much of Gunn's strength comes from his preparedness to try and make
honest poetry out of his reflections on interpersonal experience. The
results of this are often coarse and unprofound, and Gunn's evident
embarrassment at some of the more basic kinds of sexual discovery
sometimes suggests a real limitation of sensibility. But this in turn seems
to be reinforced by Gunn's crude poetic diction and clumsy reliance on
traditional metres which deny natural speech-rhythms and encourage
the side-step into declamation and poetic clowning. With his recent
switch to syllabic forms (itself only a surface tactic, of course, and no
real solution) Gunn has evaded this particular problem, and in at least
one of these later poems ("The Feel of Hands") allows a poetry to
emerge which, in feeling at least, is refreshing and genuine.

Charles Tomlinson is interesting as a heritor of poets like Eliot and
Stevens at their most philosophical: his poems are a total fusion of
reflection and experience, abstract and concrete, and he is obviously
aiming for the kind of thing that Hart Crane called "absolute" poetry.
But the overall tone is grey, with none of Crane's own summer-
lightning quality. Tomlinson has the good ear that this kind of poetry
requires, but his own poems seem over-elaborately composed and to
lack any real sense of urgency or of why it is that others have such a
sense. A poem needs to be a notch more powerful than Tomlinson's
to get away with addressing words to Van Gogh like "Farewell, and
for your instructive frenzy / Gratitude". One sees what Tomlinson
means, but Van Gogh is still with us. Above all there is a deadening
absence of other people in these poems most of the time. Tomlinson's
style is potentially fertile, but to see it turned to conflicts which were

more emotional and less directly metaphysical might be a lot more interesting than the poems he has so far given us.

My concern, then, has not been with the poets in this anthology so much as with the claims of its Introduction. I have tried to give some kind of content to the idea of a "new seriousness" and to suggest what, if anything, constitutes the essential modernness of modern poetry. But it is also necessary to remember what constitutes the essential poeticness of any poetry: we must see how little has changed as well as how much. The modern awareness of English poetry since Eliot is prefigured in such poets as Blake, Coleridge, Baudelaire and the French symbolists far more significantly than (as we have been taught) in the metaphysicals of the seventeenth century. The poetry of this tradition springs from the conflict between the artist's vision and the frustrations of the social order around him, and in modern times has had to deal increasingly with the fragmentation that has beset this social order through its loss of faith in its own necessity. The conflict and fragmentation continues to increase, and the increasingly desperate search for an underlying harmony explains why, in Blackmur's words, "our own age is specially sensitive to dream as the key to a hidden reality". But modernness cannot require us to abandon art for crude expressionism and a direct concern with violence and breakdown. "It is a terrific problem that faces the poet today", Hart Crane once wrote,

> —a world that is so in transition from a decayed culture towards a re-organisation of human evaluations that there are few common terms, general denominators of speech that are solid enough or that ring with any vibration or spiritual conviction. The great mythologies of the past (including the Church) are deprived of enough façade to even launch good raillery against. Yet much of their traditions are operative still—in millions of chance combinations of related and unrelated detail, psychological reference, figures of speech, precepts, etc. These are all a part of our common experience and the terms, at least partially, of that very experience when it defines or extends itself.
>
> The deliberate program, then, of a "break" with the past or tradition seems to me to be a sentimental fallacy . . .

In the first issue of *the Review* Donald Davie was referred to as advocating a "new aestheticism", as against Alvarez's "new serious-ness". In their discussion (see p. 157) they often found themselves in agreement and moving in and out of each other's positions, despite their differences over actual poems. This was not really surprising, because aestheticism and seriousness merge in the definition of poetry, and only debased and one-sided interpretations have seemed to keep them apart. Aestheticism, in our very empiricist British thinking, has come to stand for trivial amusement quite contingent to the real business of life; seriousness, by contrast, seems to mean the rejection of such gentility in the name of some kind of breakthrough back into what really matters. I would agree with Davie when he implies that we need a new poetry of contemplation, if this means less raw emotion and more finished poems. But such contemplation must be reached by overcoming conflicts, not by avoiding them: only in this way is poetry a serious re-creation of meaning which transcends the disorder it springs from. Crane, again, describing his own conception of poetry, wrote that:

> It is my hope to go through the combined materials of the poem, using our "real" world somewhat as a spring-board, and to give the poem as a whole an orbit or predetermined direction of its own. I would like to establish it as free from my own personality as from any chance evaluation on the reader's part. (This is, of course, an impossibility, but it is a characteristic worth mentioning.) Such a poem is at least a stab at a truth, and to such an extent may be differentiated from other kinds of poetry and called "absolute". Its evocation will not be toward decoration or amusement, but rather toward a state of consciousness, an "innocence" (Blake) or absolute beauty. In this condition there may be discoverable under new forms certain spiritual illuminations, shining with a morality essentialised from experience directly, and not from previous precepts or preoccupations. It is as though a poem gave the reader as he left it a single, new word, never before spoken and impossible to actually enunciate, but self-evident as an active principle in the reader's consciousness henceforward.

It seems to me that this defines not just one kind of poetry but what is essential in all modern poetry and all the greatest poetry of the past. Aestheticism and seriousness are reconciled in this definition; dreams and responsibilities come together. If we want a slogan it could perhaps be "Towards a New Lyricism"; but this would mean a lyricism of our total experience in which poetry assumes its full rôle as the origin and continuous re-creation of our morality and understanding. If we achieve this the lesson of Eliot will have been learned. One will be left still with the intolerable wrestle with words and meanings, but the poetry will matter.
the Review No. 2

JOHN FULLER

THOM GUNN

Faber's reissue of *Fighting Terms** (first published in 1954 by the Fantasy Press) is most welcome. Though it can hardly have been consciously designed to compensate for the disappointment of *My Sad Captains*, this reappearance of Gunn's early work does much to restore some kind of basic faith in this talented but not impeccable poet.

In this first book Gunn revealed himself above all as a love poet, an astute worrier of his own tough sensibility; sharply aware of the poses and stratagems of lust. Vigour and clarity had at last begun to be more fashionable at that time, but Gunn was sinewy and literary too (literary in a traditional and even, for then, an antique manner, not with the post-war Oxford irony of Amis or Wain) and the result was that oddly effective voice of his, a mixture of the Jacobean and the colloquial which took flatness in its stride without too often appearing typically fiftyish:

> You are not random picked. I tell you you
> Are much like one I knew before, that died.
> Shall we sit down, and drink and munch a while
> —I want to see if you will really do:
> If not we'll get it over now outside.

Gunn often used war as a metaphor for love: a glib enough trope, giving us more seventeenth century clues about the style of these early poems. It was thoroughly and convincingly done, however, and appeared to be something all his own ("Captain in Time of Peace", "The Beach Head" and so on). In many of the poems there were other metaphors as extensively used: a possible lover to be looked over like a shop or a past affair as an image of a garden. But even where Gunn departed from the military, the sense of antagonism in sexual relations was never far away. Often we were aware of a division between affection and sex; there seemed to be so much skirmishing and hard work about it all because there was always that "risk that your mild

* *Fighting Terms*. By Thom Gunn. (Faber & Faber. 1962.)

liking turn to loathing". He was not bitter, certainly not really evasive about this and hardly ever sly; nor did the self-awareness preclude wholeheartedness. Gunn, indeed, even at a time of much clever writing was notably inventive and assured.

One can now see more clearly in this first collection, however, something of that likeliness to disappoint which mars *A Sense of Movement* where attention was sharply attracted, perhaps especially on a verbal level, but the poem as a whole was often not finally convincing. Of course, in his second book Gunn had moved from emotional particularities of love to philosophical generalities of behaviour and action (very broadly speaking) and this quality is thus only marginally detectable in *Fighting Terms*, from which a good poem, the sonnet "Lerici", perhaps illustrates something of what is meant:

> Shelley was drowned near here. Arms at his side
> He fell submissive through the waves, and he
> Was but a minor conquest of the sea:
> The darkness that he met was nurse not bride.

This is a fine opening: it is bold, imaginative and, in the style perhaps of Allen Tate's "Mr. Pope", seems to promise some striking central criticism of the poet. That the development of the sonnet is away from Shelley towards the significance of the various reactions of drowning men need not in itself disappoint us, but does so, partly because the sonnet, though elegant and finished, loses its initial impact:

> Others make gestures with arms open wide,
> Compressing in the minute before death
> What great expense of muscle and of breath
> They would have made if they had never died.

These lines, completing the octave, bring us back with a bump to the low tension of the explanatory style so common in the Fifties. Interest is maintained, but excitement is lost. The second reason for disappointment is the final meaning of the piece. Here is the sestet:

> Byron was worth the sea's pursuit. His touch
> Was masterful to water, audience
> To which he could react until an end.
> Strong swimmers, fishermen, explorers: such
> Dignify death by thriftless violence—
> Squandering all their little left to spend.

One has learnt to make the sexual application, but even metaphorically the argument of the sonnet has a kind of lameness. It is still a good poem; by no means the best he can do, but a sort of average, and illustrates this weakness fairly. He does not so much "go wrong" as raise expectations with a bold opening which has little to do with the demands of shapeliness and sense that might have appeared fashionable criteria. In *A Sense of Movement* the discrepancy is often such that one finds oneself demanding a more cogent or attractive "moral", a development no doubt encouraged by Gunn's subject matter. It became more contemporary, more characteristic, just as his attitude became less sympathetic. An instance is the poem about Elvis Presley, whose pose is a stance ". . . which . . . may be posture for combat". Combat against what, we ask? What is the real significance of Presley? Or is the poet off on some erotic sidetrack, a piece of disguised butch-ery? One need not multiply examples of ambivalence about the motorcyclists and sadists in some of these poems. Indeed, all this might be thought petty. One is so often concerned merely with periodic vicissitudes of style that one tends to slide over the material of the poet's art as being somehow beyond rebuke. This is a danger. It would also be a danger to condemn attitudes out of hand. Here the point is (and it is perhaps the main criticism of Gunn's development) that the poet does not seem to be plainly enough saying what he wants to say. One would not even mind a body of verse which went beyond this rather conscious imagery of brutality or promiscuity into some plainly immoral creed. "Morality" would become irrelevant with more integrity. With individual exceptions, of course, it came to appear that Gunn was losing some central power of blending matter and manner. His Donnean candour and involvement became dissipated by evasiveness, irrelevancies and a frequently pedantic tone.

One supposes that this development is closely connected with the growth of philosophising in his poetry. It is not that he did not continue to objectify (his material was various: the Wolf Boy, Merlin, Jesus, and so on) but he did not reach to any very great heights of imagination. In *Fighting Terms* there was much more evidence of a fluid and exciting mind. In "The Wound", Gunn is powerfully in one of his most successful moods:

> The huge wound in my head began to heal
> About the beginning of the seventh week.

Its valleys darkened, its villages became still:
For joy I did not move and dared not speak;
Not doctors would cure it, but time, its patient skill.

And constantly my mind returned to Troy.
After I sailed the seas I fought in turn
On both sides, sharing even Helen's joy
Of place, and growing up—to see Troy burn—
As Neoptolemus, that stubborn boy.

I lay and rested as prescription said.
Manoeuvred with the Greeks, or sallied out
Each day with Hector. Finally my bed
Became Achilles' tent, to which the lout
Thersites came reporting numbers dead.

I was myself: subject to no man's breath:
My own commander was my enemy.
And while my belt hung up, sword in the sheath,
Thersites shambled in and breathlessly
Cackled about my friend Patroclus' death.

I called for armour, rose, and did not reel.
But, when I thought, rage at his noble pain
Flew to my head, and turning I could feel
My wound break open wide. Over again
I had to let those storm-lit valleys heal.

What is the wound, one wonders? It is incidentally interesting to note a
strong riddle element in *Fighting Terms*. A poem like "Without a
Counterpart" is almost wholly like a riddle:

I lay, peering as best I could, then saw
Two reed-lined ponds, reflections of the sky.
I noticed with a shock a long volcano
Which like a third brimmed-full with darkness lay . . .

But this is because it is physical. In other poems, including "The
Wound", the riddle element is more complex. One could really only
use the term where the demand for solution asserts itself above the
symbolic structure. Any solution one might give here is plagued by
paradox. If the state of health is self-sufficiency ("I was myself: subject
to no man's breath") one might conclude that the wound is love, or

at least the weakness which the subject of the poem feels he incurs by the bestowing of affection and interest upon another person. But Achilles in retirement was thought to be effeminate. One could hardly be convalescing in the face of Thersites' gibes about Patroclus. By locating the body of the poem in the Trojan war, Gunn has given us a subtle background of love, honour and reputation. Act Three, Scene Three, of *Troilus and Cressida* is relevant here; especially:

> *Achil.* I see my reputation is at stake;
>   My fame is shrewdly gor'd.
> *Patr.*   O, then, beware;
>   Those wounds heal ill that men do give themselves.

Another subtlety is that inaction and emotion, though harmful to ambition, are not entirely without honour ("rage at his noble pain"). The wound indeed heals badly: Patroclus's death reminds Achilles of his love, and the wound breaks open. But Hector's death could hardly be called noble.

It would be impertinent to explore any further in such forced exegesis. In themselves, these Trojan stanzas, though usefully complex and suggestive, are not poetically impeccable. There is nothing in them better than Gunn's usual style in the volume, and in some places (for example, in the second stanza) there is even a certain awkwardness.

The controlling imaginative idea of the poem is the landscape metaphor for the wound, "those storm-lit valleys". In the very next poem in the book, "Here Come the Saints", he just fails with a make-weight climax, too coolly, one might say, taking his Breughel out of Auden:

> . . . with abrupt and violent
> Motions into the terrible dark wood they go.

Here, in "The Wound", are traces of the origin of his metaphorical technique in Auden, but the effect is not too Audenesque, and apart from the second line which actually is a little empty, a sort of Biblical colouring, this framing image is splendidly done. The poem is typical Gunn: the idea is central, and the treatment shows his uncommon powers (though these are not everywhere highly sustained). The point to be drawn is that there is imagination here, and that although, as we have seen, Gunn can disappoint, he nevertheless has this power still at his disposal. It can be seen in *My Sad Captains* in a poem like "The Feel of Hands", but on the whole I found that in this collection the bold writing begins to be little compensation for the deadening coarseness and sadness of the sexual poems. Further, there is a growing indistinctness and abstraction of language (Francophilia?) which does not marry happily with the noticeable American influence. Here, for instance, it is the diction as well as the syllabics which seems unnatural and unprofitable:

> My body trots semblably
> on Market Street. I control
> that thick and singular spy,
> from a hovering planet: I
> contemplate new laws meanwhile

Gunn has chosen to omit from the version printed in his book the information that the poem was composed after taking mescalin, and perhaps this is as well. Other landscapes and grotesqueries in the latest American manner fill the second part of *My Sad Captains*. The best of them ("Blackie, the Electric Rembrandt" and "A Trucker") are, say, as good as good Corso, but one is slightly discomfited, as though Gunn had dyed his hair. Altogether, one feels he is moving fast away from the native English vigour of *Fighting Terms*, and not writing as well as he can. No doubt his next collection will be a severe test.

the Review No. 1

GRAHAM MARTIN

ROY FULLER

This* ought to be a more impressive collection than it is—Fuller is a capable and serious writer; of the two hundred or so poems collected from about twenty-five years' writing, there is no real dross, a large number of good poems, and a few better than that. It's not easy to see why as a volume it doesn't make a more distinct impression. Fuller is not, for instance, the product of any movement or "school". (The two strong influences on his work—Auden in the early poems, plus Yeats in the later—are dominant in other poets today (e.g. Larkin and Gunn) but not in the 1944-55 period when nearly half of the poems in this volume first appeared.) Repetitiveness within a narrow range of feeling has something to do with it, but not enough: you read on, nonetheless, on the lookout for the fully-achieved memorable poems the general level leads you to expect. Nor is it any overt lack of "experience", or a flight from what the last decades have offered. Though he despairs of the public world, he has nothing but scorn for contemporaries who have given up trying to cope:

> About us lie our elder writers,
> Small, gritty, barren, like detritus:
> Resistance to the epoch's rage
> Has not survived their middle age.
> The type of ivory tower varies
> But all live in the caves of caries.

Or who have never begun to try:

> The younger men, not long from mother,
> Write articles about each other,
> Examining in solemn chorus,
> Ten poems, or a brace of stories.   (1949)

Possibly he over-values the fruitfulness of "resistance to the epoch's rage" in his own work. It sometimes reads like Yeats's envy of the "heavily-built Falstaffian man" who "came cracking jokes of Civil

*Collected Poems, 1936-1960. Roy Fuller. (Andre Deutsch. 1962.)

War"; or the guilty intellectual socialist's longing for contact with "real people".

One main trouble is, I think, that Fuller has never found a wholly personal voice. Instead, he has a style. This emerged in the 1944 volume, and from then on the poems are assured and fluent, the poet fully, it seems, in command. But, if there is such a thing, it's an approximate style. There is always a constant (and even a chosen?) distance between the meanings it achieves and the meanings which, after a while, you begin to feel are missing. And this remains true, despite a steady development and growth still going on—see the section of post-1957 poems. Many of the most inward and characteristic poems seem as if written from the same obscure unchanged centre of half-explored pain, so that, collectively, they read like a series of palliative soothings of a chronic disease. Perhaps complete "cure", i.e. a real plumbing of the creative distress, would mean no more poems. Perhaps some half-recognised fear of this (where would I be without my interesting symptoms?) prevents the really satisfactory poems being written (but ensures a steady flow of unsatisfactory ones). The truth, writes Fuller, is "half-feeling and half style, / And feeling and no style is vile". In his own history, style seems a product of a continual flight from the real nature of feeling: the two halves continue to chase each other round the same beaten track.

To be more specific. Many poems show a familiar structure (it is nearly a formula)—an event has occurred, something seen, heard or read; it provokes reflections, or helps the poet identify a hitherto evasive inner experience. This is the almost invariable movement— from observed to observer, from an outer to an inner reality, and only a few poems make the return journey. Poems of this kind can (and do) fail in three ways: by not making a convincing symbolism between event and response, by not having any interesting ideas or inner experiences, or by not recording well the event or place which begins the poem. The last may sound minor, but in practice it can be more damaging than the others. Unless the poet can and does present the situation from which the poem takes off, he ought in honesty to leave it out altogether and write lyrics. This tension between event and response is, in the end, crucial to the reality of such poems.

It is here that Fuller's style is so faulty. Where it needs to be observant

and exact, it is decorative and fuzzy, full of a slurring rhetoric, and with
a verse-movement too often merely "musical". In "To My Wife"
(1942) he writes:

> My lust was as precise and fierce as that of
> The wedge-headed jaguar and the travelling Flaubert.

But what could be more precise than "I wanted you"? Certainly not
these analogies, or expansive rhythms; "lust", in any case, is one of
those unusable words, which should be forcibly retired. The lines are
immediately preceded by:

> It was no vague nostalgia which I breathed
> Between the purple colloids of the air:
> My lust, etc. . . .

a phrase that sounds quite pleasant till you find that a colloid is either
"a sticky gelatinous substance having the consistency of glue", or "a
non-crystalloid state of substance in suspension in water or alcohol
which does not diffuse through parchment or a collodion membrane".
He seems lucky to have been able to breathe at all.

This is an early poem, and a bad example, but, though in more subtle
ways, writing "cardinal" where "red" would do (see "Jag and Hang-
over") is a constant practice.

> A final revelation—
> The image of a sea-bird
> With scimitars of wings
> Pathetic feet tucked away,
> A fine ill-omened name,
> Sweeping across the grey.
> "The Emotion of Fiction" (1944)

Why are the feet "pathetic"? "Scimitars" may give the rough shape of
the wings, and again it sounds good, but it gives too much else as
well—what are the wings likely to cut? (surely not the air); are they
really shiny and hard? If not, why are they made to seem so? And
wouldn't it be better to know the bird's name, instead of being offered
vague emotions about it? The questions may seem too prescriptive, but
I think these lines from Yeats justify them:

> But soon a tear-drop started up,
> For aimless joy had made me stop

> Beside the little lake
> To watch a white gull take
> A bit of bread thrown up into the air;
> Now gyring down and perning there
> He splashed where an absurd
> Portly green-pated bird
> Shook off the water from his back;
> Being no more demoniac
> A stupid happy creature
> Could rouse my whole nature.
>
> "Demon and Beast"

You can enter into this situation on your own terms as well as on Yeats'; but with Fuller's lines his is the only permitted response, so that you feel he is using the situation to put something over on you. In yet another case, he seems to be putting it over on himself as well:

> again I see
> How still the world belongs to the obtuse
> And passionate, and that the bosom's small
> But noticeable curve subtends its tall
> Explosions and orations of mad abuse.
>
> "The Perturbation of Uranus" (1957)

The poet is recording the immediate physical attraction of a girl in a coffee bar, and contrasting its implications with those of a book he is reading (which stresses the priority mind must have) in the "future of the breed". There is the same vagueness: "small / But noticeable curve"—does he mean shallow, or perhaps slight? A girl's breast-curve that is actually small would be noticeable in a way that he doesn't mean; or if the girl is pubescent this gives "noticeable" yet another unsupported inflection. Whatever the meaning, a "small curve" is still badly observed. There is also the shift into irrational metaphor ("subtends"), and well-sounding decorative phrases, both part of a blurring process at work in the whole poem. Earlier in the verse, there is the uneasy circling as he glances "occasionally where the urn / Distorts the image of her whom I confirm / Is not distorted . . ." It seems reasonable to conclude that writing like this helps the poet to talk about a state of feeling without really "declaring his interest".

The poem's theme is that girls have this power to disturb "the learned men" from their vision of a good world (somewhat sketchily indicated in "virtuous laws and golden hives"); but *only* if the intellectual sublimate their desires into vision, art and learning can the "short degraded lives" of the "obtuse and passionate" be very enjoyable. In a word, the learned deny their instinct so that the obtuse don't have to. As one of the learned himself, everything depends on how disinterestedly the poet uses this idea. I find Fuller's use disturbing—portentous about the learned and their sacrifices; patronising and envious about those stupid enough to be able to enjoy the simple life of instinct and emotion. In terms of its feeling, it could be a poem about the failure to make the sublimation, but it means to be the opposite. There is the smooth competence of the writing, and there is this damaging incoherence: the two seem in fact to be logically connected.

"The Perturbation of Uranus" belongs to a series of reflective sententious poems more or less defective in this way: the thought cloaks feelings much less intricate or intricate in the wrong way. The ample Ciceronian manner conceals the "fault". The poems least affected are in the 1944 volume, but there the better observation is balanced by duller thoughts. In "The Plains", the poet describes the African veld by day as innocent and beautiful, but by night as violent and ruthless, to conclude next morning that the life of nature has no moral content. The irritating thing here is the air of having proved something. A better poem of this type is "The Giraffes" where the thought is offered more tentatively: the description simply concludes with nightfall when "cold and dark now bring the image of / Those creatures walking without pain or love"—the suggestion being all the more powerful for not having been hammered out of the creature, detail by detail.

Fuller's best poems use events to symbolise a state of mind, rather than as occasions for little sermons. Another 1944 poem, "The Statue", illustrates this group: it contrasts an equestrian statue in an African port—symbol of power, of a certain history, and of art—with the figure of a man smoking a pipe, and looking at his feet, as he squats on deck waiting for the ship to enter the harbour. The poet decides that the latter image is the best symbol for the city, and despite some easy feeling which can be felt in the movement of the lines, the real tension between the two images survives:

> As though there dominated this sea's threshold and this night
> Not the raised hooves, the thick snake neck, the profile and the night,

The wrought, eternal bronze, the dead protagonist, the fight,
But that unmoving, pale but living shape that drops no tears,
Ridiculous and haunting, which each epoch reappears,
And is what history is not. O love, O human fears!

This preoccupation with art—identified here with the violence of
history, and with government, over against humanity—provides, I
think, a more significant clue to his work as a whole. It is more and
more prominent in the later poems, both as view and as subject-matter.
One stress derives from the Thirties: the poet must write for an audience
with a shared public world in mind; he must be intelligible, and must
make sure that his work is neither irrelevant nor reactionary
the times may be hard but that does not justify a refusal to face them.
In this mood, he even quotes a memorable letter by Coleridge to
Wordsworth: "I wish you would write in blank verse, addressed to
those who, in consequence of the complete failure of the French
Revolution, have thrown up all hopes of the amelioration of mankind,
and are sinking into an almost epicurean selfishness, disguising the same
under the soft titles of domestic attachment and contempt for visionary
philosophes." I don't know any other poet of recent times serious enough
both in his despair and in his hope to reach back in this way for the
relevant period in English poetry. And when one remembers the date
in which Fuller most strongly asserts the poet's social responsibility—
1948-56—the period in which the authoritative trend was running so
strongly in the opposite direction, the tenacity and independence of
this attitude becomes clear. But to assert is not the same as to define.
What the poet's social responsibility *is* is far from clear; or where clear,
so brusque and political that it doesn't argue for much real faith in the
social necessity of art. "Expostulation and Inadequate Reply", the
poem which uses the Coleridge letter for epigraph, even seems to
envisage a good world without art, and art merely as an element in the
difficult history of effort, relapse and recovery, by which men struggle
into the artless future: "the new, / Delicate but sure republic of the
crocus". Possibly, in a poem about personal weakness—the "inadequate
reply" of the title—it is wrong to worry its general concept, but the
two are not unconnected. Fuller's insistence on the social responsibility
of the artist seems to be more of his will than of his reason.

The other stress is Freudian, and is the truer centre. But it leads to an odd conclusion. In Freud, art is as means to end: the enjoyment of the reality ("honour, riches, the love of women") from which his neurosis excludes the artist, but which he re-enters with the help of his—as it turns out, socially-rewarding—symptoms, his art. Fuller accepts the analysis of art's motive impulse, of the artist as a man in some way shut off from direct enjoyment of life, and of art as the product of this exclusion, but not the clear-cut Freudian view of reality. (Neither, admittedly, does Freud in other places.) Art is far from clear. Sometimes it is personal therapy, or consolation, sometimes it has the long-term socially valuable results of vision. But there is never a feeling that it returns the artist to satisfaction in life itself. Most usually, there is no answer, and the problem takes the shape of uneasy self-consciousness about what he, the poet, is doing in writing poems: in one sense he knows, but in another he doesn't. Contrast Yeats: "But what cared I that set him on to ride, / I, starved from the bosom of his faery bride?" Even as late as this, this is knowledge to Yeats, and it releases him—the poem itself seems to release him—into acceptance of a new self. "I must lie down where all the ladders start / In the foul rag-and-bone shop of the heart". But in Fuller the knowledge of motive only extends his self-mistrust to the very act of writing. His use of language is one of the results—the rhetoric which is a kind of private magic, the inaccuracy, and the disguise.

"Amateur Film-Making" is the best of several poems which find the right image for Fuller's deeply uncertain feeling about art, and so about himself as poet. It begins by describing a film: the poet and a friend are walking in a wood on a damp afternoon. The friend is making a film of the poet "posed on various backgrounds", and the poem recounts the choosing of one of these. To the friend it is picturesque in a way that we see as gimmicky. To the poet it has a further meaning which the poem reveals. The irony is delicate and cutting: the friend is an amateur artist, filming a real artist in an obviously "popular" way. (It would do nicely for *The Queen*.) The real artist then writes a poem about being filmed as an artist. The poem images the real artist's perception of what, really, is going on: he half enjoys this sort of posing; he also sees what else it involves. Here are the important lines:

> You say: "This is ideal: I'll pan along
> The horizontal trunks and you, near me,

Will be standing by the biggest of the roots
The shot will end with you in close-up, leaning
Gently on your stick, expressionless, against
The complicated tendrils, stones, dried clay,
         Of the upturned root."

The root is like a monstrous withered flower,
A Brobdingnagian mole or tumour, or
Some product of the microscopic eye
Of a romantic painter; and I stand
Beside it . . .

"I'm shooting now," you say. "Prepare your face."
The camera purrs; you swivel slowly round,

. . . And finally I face the little eye—
Behind it yours, which watches in the glass
         The impersonal image.

"I'm holding this," you say . . .

This seems to me a very fine poem, and if I wanted to represent Fuller by one poem this would be it. Somewhere near the centre of all of his writing, but rarely focussed so clearly, there is this final emphasis on life as grotesque and terrible. Reason (or neurosis) barely control its menace, so barely that even though all specifically human life depends on it, the control seems to him not far short of pointless. It is this vision that shuts the artist out of directly satisfying life, that drives him to art; but since art is one of the questionable activities on which human life depends, the meaning of the vision saps continuously at the value of his activity as artist. "Amateur Film-Making" catches with rare accuracy just this balance, or bias rather, of attitudes.

There is one other group of poems, successful in a related, though less interesting way: "Meditation", "The Lake", "The Civilization", in which the central feeling provides a more substantial link with Auden, aspects of MacNiece (and even with Angus Wilson). It is an energy of utter hopelessness, of almost exulting desperation. "Again the driver / Pulls on his gloves and in a blinding snowstorm starts / Upon his deadly journey, and again the writer runs howling to his art". Fuller is never so splendidly energetic as that, but he can strike the genuine "waiting-for-the-end" note with its expressed core of hysteria. I find these poems better than evasively rhetorical efforts at managing or "accepting" or being philosophical about this state of mind. The order they achieve is less fine than that of a poem like "Amateur Film-Making", but it is genuine. Again the date is interesting: the three I've mentioned are all in the 1954 volume, i.e. were written at the height of the Cold War. Subsequently, Fuller seems to have withdrawn into a more personal world—he can hardly lack other occasions for poems of doom—indicated by the series "Mythological Sonnets, To My Son", where his despair is given more general form, and I think this is a pity. On the other hand, "The Ides of March" uses the dramatic persona, as do the "Faustian Sketches"; and there is a move towards the particularisation that he seems to find so hard.

Finally, though Fuller is to me a more interesting poet than, say, Graves, it's not easy to forget that he seems to lack Graves' faith that poems are worth writing, and worth the hard slog that goes into every line Graves finally releases. At the end of the 1954 volume he tries in a short poem to rebut the objection that his "verses are depressing / Obsessed with years and death". But it is he and not his verses that shows obsession. A good two-thirds of his artistic skill seems devoted to keeping the obsession out by calling it something else—myth, philosophy, gloomy wisdom—or by putting it in rhetorical terms, which is still an unbeatable way of ruining good poems. Fuller learned it early, and too well.

the Review No. 3

IAN HAMILTON

ROBERT LOWELL

The title of Robert Lowell's best-known book, *Lord Weary's Castle*, was cleverly chosen. The ballad of Lambkin tells how Lord Weary hired a mason to build him a castle and, when the job was done, refused to pay him for it. The mason took his revenge by breaking into the castle and murdering Lord Weary's wife and child. Ingratitude, exploitation, the indefensible failure of obligation to God that man is guilty of and must be violently punished for, these are pervasively the concerns of Lowell's early verse.

A Bostonian turned Catholic, it is with some relish that Lowell imagines the torments of hell prefigured in terms of the locale whose traditions he is out to revile; there is a sense in which he sees himself as the nurse who let the wronged mason into Lord Weary's Castle. Lowell's Catholicism has been well described as simply a way of abusing Calvinism and in his most consciously scathing assaults on fallen Boston it does fall into an extrinsic rôle, becomes not much more than a convenient and rather decorative position to attack from. It is no cure for the ills it helps to diagnose.

Like Jonathan Edwards, whose biography Lowell once started to write and on whose works some poems are explicitly based, he can make "chimneys suddenly leap into flame in the midst of a revival meeting". Boston is part of hell,

> disgrace
> Elbows about our windows in this planned
> Babel of Boston where our money talks
> And multiplies the darkness. . . .

its streets are "hell-fire streets", its adulterers grow scales like the serpent in Eden, its waters are "fouled with the blue sailors", victims not only of war, but also of Quaker profiteering. It is that "lack of common consistency" which Melville found in the Quaker Captain Peleg that is the subject of Lowell's central early poem, *The Quaker*

Graveyard in Nantucket, ostensibly an elegy for a dead relative but, more deeply, a bitter appraisal of New England morality:

> Though refusing, from conscientious scruples, to bear arms against land invaders, yet himself had illimitably invaded the Atlantic and Pacific; and though a sworn foe to human bloodshed, yet had he in his straight-bodied coat, spilled tuns upon tuns of leviathan gore ... very probably he had long since come to the sage and sensible conclusion that a man's religion is one thing, and this practical world quite another. This world pays dividends.

By relating Ahab's whaleboats to the North Atlantic fleet (Lowell was a conscientious objector to World War II), he is as much concerned to express his hatred of war as of a hypocritic pacifism, but if one recalls the tablets on the walls of the Whaleman's Chapel in *Moby Dick*, and Melville's description of the Nantucketers as "like so many Alexanders", who have "overrun and conquered the watery world", there can be little doubt as to where the emphasis lies. Nor can there be any mistaking the manner: it is substantially that of Father Mapple who, "when describing Jonah's sea-storm, seemed tossed by a storm himself", and who although enjoying a "wide reputation for sincerity and sanctity" is yet open to suspicion of "courting notoriety by ... mere tricks of the stage".

Grotesqueries are frequent in these early poems—in one, a dead ancestor of Lowell's is met by a Christ who walks across the water of Boston's public gardens to take him "beyond Charles River to the Acheron"; in another, the Virgin's "scorched, blue thunderbreasts of love" are asked to "pour buckets of blessings on my burning head". Lowell's puns ("torn-up tilestones crown the victor") come from the same malignant source and they are so recognisably part of his manner that when one encounters, in *Poems* 1938-49, what is probably a misprint—a reference to a corpse's "heel-bent deity" (it's "hell-bent" in the American edition)—one cannot be entirely sure, since a few lines back there are some "heel-headed dogfish", that a pun is not intended. This is not as trivial as it might sound. Lowell is a clotted and extremely difficult writer in these early poems—there are whole passages which seem to make no sense at all—and if one is to work at him one needs some guarantee that he is not prone to mere ingenuities. (For example, is there a meaningful relation between the "heavy lids" of the sea-gulls in *The Quaker Graveyard in Nantucket* and the "heavy eye-lids" ot Our

B*

Lady of Walsingham in the same poem? There could be, of course, but what matters is that a signalled relation is not developed beyond that point where the author might justifiably be suspected of either slovenliness or casual dexterity.)

Lowell's obscurity too rarely seems to be founded on long hard effort to be understood. It arises most often where his subject is explicitly Christian. It is not so much that there are recondite Christian references —though these are plentiful enough—but that the language at such points is at its most thoughtlessly vulgar and sensational:

> O Christ, the spiralling years
> Slither with child and manger to a ball
> Of ice; and what is man? We tear our rags
> To hang the Furies by their itching ears,
> And the green needles nail us to the wall.

The assurance with which the elements of this situation are so precisely named (it is a *ball of ice* that is *slithered to*, specifically and not just that the spiralling years, say, *spiral to ice*) seems to invite the reader to "picture" what is going on, implying that such a picturing procedure will yield more significance than could be provoked by bare, analytic statement. And yet is the "picture" one can most charitably conjure from these clues anything more than bemusing and pointlessly grotesque, and quite inadequate to give force to the rhetorical question it inaugurates? The right to throw out portentous queries like "what is man?" cannot be lightly claimed and here it is apparent that the poet really doesn't *mean* any more than what, if anything, that question means: he has been only half-attending to the conceivable limits of his words' reverberations. In his many self-indulgent performances of this sort, Lowell seems as much at the mercy of his words' sound and savagery as the reader.

His ear is no more faultless than his tact. His densely alliterative iambic line, its persistent enjambment blocked by compulsively heavy rhyming, too often solidifies into a monotonously high-pitched rhetoric of desperation which can be repellent, particularly where the sense is elusive:

> Under St. Peter's bell the parish sea
> Swells with its smelt into the burlap shack
> Where Joseph plucks his hand-lines like a harp,
> And hears the fearful *Puer natus est*

> Of circumcision, and relieves the wrack
> And howls of Jesus whom he holds. How sharp
> The burden of the Law before the beast:
> Time and the grindstone and the knife of God.
> The child is born in blood, O child of blood.

The words are harsh enough—"wrack", "howls", "beast", "knife", etc.—and there is evidently energy at work amongst them, but it is an energy that seems bent on increasing their volume without sharpening their point. Finally, the effect is of dullness and even staginess. The poet has put all his money on the individual distinctness and force of his tone of voice, he appears to have trusted that the compulsive pressure of what can be feebly described as "the personal note" (as opposed to, say, "the personal fact", "the personal situation") will suffice to particularise a traditionally "evocative" vocabulary and a crudely gratuitous alliterative tread. Now and again, in Lowell, this can seem to happen, but rarely without some supporting advance in concentration, clarity and particularisation. In Part 2 of *The Quaker Graveyard in Nantucket*, for example, his subject is the violent confrontation of the Quaker by the retributive energy of the sea, his properties are drawn from local and literary New England sources and organised so as to give density and pointed resonance to a trained personal experience. In these circumstances, Lowell's vocabulary is held just this side of its characteristically florid crush, and his alliteration is sensitively devised so that in the running battle it sets up between, broadly, the "s", "sh", "w" sounds of the sea and the "p", "b" sounds of resistance to the sea, it contrives—for all its hearty obtrusiveness—a spectacular auditory support to the poem's statement:

> Whenever winds are moving and their breath
> Heaves at the roped-in bulwark of this pier,
> The terns and sea-gulls tremble at your death
> In these home-waters. Sailor, can you hear
> The Pequod's sea-wings, beating landward, fall
> Headlong and break on our Atlantic wall
> Off 'Sconset, where the yawing S-boats splash
> The bell-buoy, with ballooning spinnakers,
> As the entangled, screeching mainsheet clears
> The blocks; off Madaket, where lubbers lash
> The heavy surf and throw their long lead squids
> For blue-fish? Sea-gulls blink their heavy lids

> Sea-ward. The winds' wings beat upon the stones,
> Cousin, and scream for you and the claws rush
> At the sea's throat and wring it in the slush
> Of this old Quaker graveyard where the bones
> Cry out in the long night for the hurt beast
> Bobbing by Ahab's whaleboats in the East.

Here overflow is inhibited by the presence of concrete facts—place-names, the cousin whose elegy it is, *Moby Dick*, the nautical terms, the S-boats and so on—but one feels that the pressure is towards a transformation or, more accurately, a wrenching of these facts into a purely emblematic or rhetorical condition. Randall Jarrell has said that Lowell sometimes doesn't "have enough trust in God and tries to do everything himself". The world is mistrusted in the same way.

The best of *Lord Weary's Castle* are those poems in which Lowell has attempted his figure of ultimate retribution and calamity with the controlling assistance of some local or literary anchor. Readers of his *Imitations* will not be surprised to find him here drawing liberally on various literary sources. In *The Quaker Graveyard in Nantucket* Melville and Thoreau are pitted against "an adaptation of several paragraphs from E. I. Watkins' *Catholic Art and Culture*". The Thoreau source is one of the innumerable pieces of useful background information that are provided in Hugh B. Staples' *Robert Lowell: The First Twenty Years*. Thoreau writes:

> I saw many marble feet and matted heads as the clothes were raised, and one livid, swollen, and mangled body of a drowned girl . . . to which some rags still adhered, with a string, half concealed by the flesh, about its swollen neck; the coiled-up wreck of a human hulk, gashed by the rocks or fishes, so that the bone and muscle were exposed, but quite bloodless—merely red and white—with wide-open and staring eyes, yet lustreless, dead-lights; or like the cabin windows of a stranded vessel, filled with sand . . .

And Lowell:

>   Light
> Flashed from his matted head and marble feet,
> He grappled at the net
> With the coiled, hurdling muscles of his thighs:
> The corpse was bloodless, a botch of reds and whites,
> Its open, staring eyes

Were lustreless dead-lights
Or cabin windows on a stranded hulk
Heavy with sand.

What is admirable here is the sensitivity with which Lowell has selected
from Thoreau's lines. By paring down the description of the corpse to
the simple "was bloodless", and by letting the weight of his presentation
fall on its "open, staring eyes", Lowell achieves a shocked impressionis-
tic vigour which Thoreau—for all his helpful qualifications—fails to
carry. Lowell intensifies where Thoreau takes his time. In the other
outstanding "literary" poems, "The Exiles Return", "After the Surprising Conversions", and "Mr. Edwards and the Spider", the same
thing occurs. Lowell lends his impassioned speaking voice to intensify
a piece of discursive prose which, in its turn, influences him to curb his
rhetoric. Where the source is itself impassioned, though, Lowell tends
to try and go one better—this is a characteristic of his *Imitations*—and
this sort of mess can result (after Villon):

> Now here, now there, the starling and the sea
> Gull splinter the groined eye-balls of my sin,
> Brothers, more beaks of birds than needles in
> The fathoms of the Bayeux Tapestry:
> God wills it, wills it, wills it: it is blood.

But by and large, Lowell's sources have been a help to him, demanding
of him both passion and objectivity. They might also have led him to
that increased respect for character and situation which marks the later
poems in *Lord Weary's Castle* and persists through *The Mills of the
Kavanaughs* (which had its first English publication as an appendix to
Mr. Staples's book) to *Life Studies*. R. P. Blackmur wrote of Lowell's
first published poetry (*Land of Unlikeness*, published in a limited edition
of 250 copies in 1944, and partly contained in *Lord Weary's Castle*): "in
dealing with men his faith compels him to be fractiously vindictive,
and in dealing with faith his experience of men compels him to be
nearly blasphemous", and it is true that in the majority of the poems in
Lord Weary's Castle, Boston exists as a moral emblem; Lowell uses its
signposts for polemical purposes but the people are nowhere to be
found. With the Jonathan Edwards poems, though, and "Between the
Porch and the Altar", a new interest in narrative emerges. The opening

lines of "Katherine's Dream", for instance, are like nothing else in *Lord Weary's Castle*:

> It must have been a Friday. I could hear
> The top-floor typist's thunder and the beer
> That you had brought in cases hurt my head;
> I'd sent the pillows flying from my bed,
> I hugged my knees together and I gasped.

But even in these, the calmest of Lowell's early lines, one can detect that debilitating antagonism between the rhetorical and the narrative motive which is to become centrally ruinous in the dramatic monologues of *The Mills of the Kavanaughs* volume. "You feel that the people are made up," Lowell has said of Browning (*Paris Review* interview, Spring 1961), "you feel there's a glaze between what he writes and what really happened", that he lacks "some kind of sympathy and observation of people". This is true of Lowell's own dramatic monologues. His advance in subject matter is not accompanied by a substantial variation of manner or broadening of emotional range. Although the Catholic symbolism is less obtrusive and some attempt is being made to take people seriously, the characters are still the horribly punished, the suicidal. They are still fallen and theological. Great poetry can get written about madness but there is no such thing as great madness. Composure must at least be looked for and it must be more integral than the mere formality which the aping of traditional verse forms can effect. With Lowell there is a sense in which even this formality is present only to be disgraced. The learned hysteria of *The Mills of the Kavanaughs* is the culmination of Lowell's apocalyptic vein (only "Falling Asleep over the Aeneid" achieves anything like the powered restraint of the best of *Lord Weary's Castle*) and with it he seems to realise that his full-blooded gestural rhetoric is too uniformly emphatic an instrument for handling the problems of narrative and too monotonously single-pitched for objective or dramatic representations of human behaviour and the sorts of secular situation in which he is becoming interested. It was perhaps considerations of this sort, together with what seems to have been Lowell's de-conversion from Roman Catholicism (recorded in "Beyond the Alps?") which brought about the radical change of style that characterises most of the verse in *Life Studies*. Searching for a "breakthrough back into life",

Lowell abandons his tight metric, indeed abandons any sort of formality of line, and writes a verse that is loose, subdued and prosaic, full of fine perceptions and richly disconsolate in tone, but, as Colin Falck has admirably pointed out (see p. 8), quite disorganised.

The autobiographical poems in *Life Studies* act as elaborations of certain characters and incidents in Lowell's prose autobiography, a fragment of which was printed alongside in the American edition. Here is some prose:

> Almost immediately he bought a larger and more stylish house; he sold his ascetic stove-black Hudson and bought a plump brown Buick; later the Buick was exchanged for a high-toned, as-good-as-new Packard with a custom-designed royal blue and mahogany body. Without drama, his earnings more or less decreased from year to year.

And here, a verse account of the same events:

> whenever he left a job,
> he bought a smarter car.
> Father's last employer
> was Scudder, Stevens and Clark, Investment Advisors,
> himself his only client.
> While Mother dragged to bed alone,
> Read Menninger,
> and grew more and more suspicious,
> he grew defiant.
> Night after night,
> *a la clarte deserte de sa lampe,*
> he slid his ivory Annapolis slide rule
> across a pad of graphs—
> piker speculations! In three years
> he squandered sixty thousand dollars.

There is no reason why the first of these passages should be set out as prose and the second syntactically line-broken into verse: indeed, the first passage acts upon the reader more "poetically"—that is, the colours and the car-names are allowed to do the work and there is none of the chattiness that distends the second. The closing comments on Father's earnings could be interchanged without anything being lost either way.

On the whole, the explicitly autobiographical poems in *Life Studies* add little except further information to the prose. It might ultimately be possible to see them as precisely the sort of low-pressure exploration of his Boston past that Lowell was in need of to lend some specific resonance to his discontent. Certainly, a recent poem like "For the Union Dead" is an encouraging sign in this direction: it shows Lowell returning to the Boston legend with an objective malice, a detail and variety of local reference and a sharpened sense of public responsibility. Henry James's remarks about Hawthorne are truer of the later than of the early Lowell:

> It is only in a country where newness and change and brevity of tenure are the common substance of life, that the fact of one's ancestors having lived for a hundred and seventy years in a single spot would become an element of one's morality. It is only an imaginative American that would feel urged to keep reverting to this circumstance, to keep analysing and cunningly considering it.

Lowell's attitude to Boston has not grown up to analysis and cunning without a considerable loss in intensity: he is now faced with the problem of recapturing something of his early vigour. The melodramatic gestures of despair that infiltrate some of his most recent poems ("I am tired. Everyone's tired of my turmoil") and run through *Imitations* are an attempt towards this end, perhaps. *Imitations* itself does not represent a significant advance: it "was written from time to time when I was unable to do anything of my own" and for all the freedom of these renderings ("from Homer to Pasternak"), their brilliant original flashes, they are, substantially, not anything of his own. One must still look to *Life Studies* for a clue to Lowell's future, to "Waking in the Blue", "Man and Wife", "Memories of West Street and Lepke" and particularly to the sort of achievement that is represented by these lines from "Home After Three Months Away". Here, what is seen is transformed but not violated by what is understood, there is an intimate collaboration of exploratory and rhetorical energies, and the measurement is by a voice that is memorably personal:

> Recuperating, I neither spin nor toil.
> Three stories down below,
> a choreman tends our coffin's length of soil,
> and seven horizontal tulips blow.
> Just twelve months ago,
> those flowers were pedigreed
> imported Dutchmen, now no one need
> distinguish them from weed.

Bushed by the late spring snow,
they cannot meet
another year's snowballing enervation.
I keep no rank or station.
Cured, I am frizzled stale and small.

EDWIN MORGAN

EDWIN MUIR

It is a world, perhaps; but there's another.

It is always interesting, and often valuable, to examine the work of a poet who is out of the main stream of his contemporaries' verse. Edwin Muir was little interested in the technical innovation and linguistic experiment that characterised the literature of his period, and his poetry failed to make much impact until, towards the end of his life, the fading of the "modern movement" allowed his plainer virtues (like those also of Robert Graves) to come into some prominence. Muir himself came late to poetry, and owing to his scrappy education had many initial difficulties to surmount, some of them difficulties a younger man might have taken in his stride in the natural excitement of discovering, following, and discarding poetic models. As he says in his *Autobiography*: "I had no training; I was too old to submit myself to contemporary influences ... Though my imagination had begun to work I had no technique by which I could give expression to it." It may fairly be said, I think, that he never did develop an entirely sure-footed technique; even his last poems are liable to be flawed by some awkward rhythm, some clumsy inversion, some flatness of vocabulary: yet by going his own way he establishes the point that what is awkward or flat is not necessarily more fatal to poetry than what is tediously admirable in accomplishment. Without wanting to praise slackness over slickness, a reader can find himself admitting that a thought-provoking piece remains a thought-provoking piece, even when its critical viability is well under proof. Muir of course has many drab, dull poems which don't come to life at all, and that is another matter. But the best of them have a quiet, persistent, winning quality which overcomes the occasional stammering of the voice.

Although in his reliance on traditional verse-forms and avoidance of startling or broken imagery Muir was out of step with his time, his search for a usable mythology links him to his contemporaries. In this very recalcitrant problem his solution is no more successful than that of Yeats, Pound, or Eliot. Instead of casting a wide net like these poets, he practised economy and restraint, relying on a narrow range of recurrent images—road and journey, labyrinth and stronghold, living and heraldic animals—and a handful of unrecondite myths in which the chief figures are Hector and Achilles, Odysseus and Penelope, Oedipus and Prometheus, Adam and Abraham. It is through such legendary and often heroic figures (supplemented now and again by such later historical characters as Knox and Calvin) and such Kafkaesque imagery (drawn frequently from his own dreams, which were at various periods of his life obsessionally powerful) that Muir projects his experience and vision of the world of time against the imagined world of eternity. But with what success?

> My childhood all a myth
> Enacted in a distant isle ...

As P. H. Butter points out in his very useful introduction to Muir's work,* Muir was the last born of a fairly large family on an Orkney farm and so grew up in a seemingly solid, secure, timelessly established environment: a glowing self-sufficient world that too readily lent itself to the myth of an Eden, once its charm had been shattered by the luckless family migration to Glasgow. The idea of Eden, a Fall, and a search for reconstituted unity and harmony is central to Muir's poetry. As an idea it is overworked, and often brought in unconvincingly, but clearly the poet was haunted all his days by the contrast between his protected Orkney boyhood and the harsh realities of industrial Glasgow he was plunged into as a youth, and a philosophy so rooted in early personal experience needs careful watching if a poet is to persuade others of its value. Muir took to myth too eagerly. His poetry would have been strengthened by a greater realism and materiality. Powerful material which he is able to make use of in his prose (e.g. his memorable description of the Fairport bone-factory in his *Autobiography*) he cannot allow into the world of his poetry. Perhaps by a natural modesty or diffidence, he seldom presents his experience directly—despite his admiration for Wordsworth—and this sometimes results in muted or shadowy effects where we feel an unexpressed resonance beating vainly

* *Edwin Muir.* Writers & Critics Series, Oliver & Boyd, Edinburgh and London, 1962.

back from the poem towards the past instead of outwards towards us. Professor Butter assumes, for example, that in the early "Ballad of Hector in Hades", which is based on a childhood recollection of being rather frighteningly chased home from school by another boy, the mythologising of the experience into the hunting of Hector by Achilles "has enabled him to objectify his personal experiences, to universalise it and make it into a work of art". But I feel on the contrary that this very Wordsworthian incident would have taught Muir more as a poet than if he had tried to say more directly and sharply what it meant or seemed to mean to him. To translate it into the terms of classical mythology is, in a poetic sense, too easy, even if the resulting poem is not a bad one.

It is only fair to add that to Muir himself the "fable" accompanied and brooded over the "story" at almost every moment of life: not only, as most obviously, in Orkney, where, as he tells us, "there was no great distinction between the ordinary and the fabulous; the lives of living men turned into legend", but later as he motored through the desolate *paysage moralisé* of the slag-hills round Glasgow:

> dwarf-like and sinister, suggesting an immeasurably shrivelled and debased second-childhood . . . I saw young men wandering in groups among these toy ranges, and the sight suddenly recalled to me the wood-cuts in *The Pilgrim's Progress* which I had read as a boy; perhaps because this scene really seemed to be more like an allegorical landscape with abstract figures than a real landscape with human beings.—*Scottish Journey*.

We must grant him the reality of this feeling, and yet we can be disappointed that he moves so quickly into the abstract, allegorical landscapes. He confesses in the *Autobiography* that "dreams go without a hitch into the fable, and waking life does not". This means in practice that his poetry does not always fully "earn" the mythology it presents. And, conversely, when Muir does want to comment on contemporary life he may be rather at a loss, wanting to mythologise but being too timid to euphemerise. Muir's chief weakness, indeed, is that he came to use Good and Evil as flags of convenience. The poem "The Good Town", for instance, leaves a melodramatic impression because one knows very well what the poet is talking about but one simply doesn't accept the "universalising" black-and-white opposition between the Danny Kaye "streets of friendly neighbours" where lock and key were "quaint antiquities fit for museums" while ivy trailed "across the prison door" and their later metamorphosis into a place where

> If you see a man
> Who smiles good-day or waves a lordly greeting
> Be sure he's a policeman or a spy.

In his *Essays on Literature and Society* Muir attacked Alexander Blok for being too responsive to historical change, but Blok could with some justice have blamed Muir for deliberately muffling his own very real responsiveness to change and for persuading himself—against all the evidence, not least the evidence of his own Christian faith—that

> Nothing can come of history but history.

What Muir felt most deeply and expressed most movingly was the sense of aftermath—the slow passage of time after some great or terrible event, the endurance or patience or suffering of survivors, the crumbling of wasted cities: Eden after the Fall, Troy after it was sacked, Penelope remembering Odysseus and Telemachos remembering Penelope, Oedipus old and blind, Prometheus on the rock and later in his grave, Abraham the wanderer, Scotland with its long annals of "wasted bravery idle as a song", the world after an atomic war. Muir's acute sense of time in its relation to action is seen in the fine "Telemachos Remembers"—

> The weary loom, the weary loom,
> The task grown sick from morn to night,
> From year to year. The treadle's boom
> Made a low thunder in the room.
> The woven phantoms mazed her sight.
>
> If she had pushed it to the end,
> Followed the shuttle's cunning song
> So far she had no thought to rend
> In time the web from end to end,
> She would have worked a matchless wrong.
>
> Instead, that jumble of heads and spears,
> Forlorn scraps of her treasure trove.
> I wet them with my childish tears
> Not knowing she wove into her fears
> Pride and fidelity and love.

—and in a larger, geological context in his remarkable poem "The Grave of Prometheus":

> Yet there you still may see a tongue of stone,
> Shaped like a calloused hand where no hand should be,
> Extended from the sward as if for alms,
> Its palm all licked and blackened as if with fire.
> A mineral change made cool his fiery bed,
> And made his burning body a quiet mound,
> And his great face a vacant ring of daisies.

In the poem "Troy" the aftermath of calamity is chosen, not the moment of destruction itself, and this gives a peculiar horror to the situation: an old Trojan warrior, gone mad, is living in the sewers under the city, fighting hordes of rats; he is discovered by a band of robbers and dragged to the surface; he sees the city like a graveyard

> With tumbled walls for tombs, the smooth sward wrinkled
> As Time's last wave had long since passed that way,
> The sky, the sea, Mount Ida and the islands,
> No sail from edge to edge, the Greeks clean gone.
> They stretched him on a rock and wrenched his limbs,
> Asking: "Where is the treasure?" till he died.

Muir's emphasis on the pointlessness of history was not always as cruel as this, but it is a theme that was never very far from his mind. Connected in part with his consciousness of a lost Eden, it also owes something to his dreams and nightmares with their fears of "eternal recurrence" and to his own lack of sympathy with contemporary history, which he saw as a series of defeats, disappointments and growing threats. There is a strand of pessimism in his reflections on human destiny which his religious hope was never quite robust enough to dismiss, and he outgrew such early belief as he had in economic and political solutions. This does not mean that the pessimism is not shot through with hope and longing, often a stoic hope and a metaphysical longing. The nightmarish poem "The Combat", based on dream material, describes an endlessly recurring fight between a powerful and an apparently defenceless animal in which the "soft brown beast" is mauled and savaged but always manages to escape and live to fight again; neither animal "loses", but

> The killing beast that cannot kill
> Swells and swells in his fury till
> You'd almost think it was despair.

One might say that if this is an image of life, of man's fate, life would hardly be worth living on such terms. Yet on second thoughts one can see history through the eyes of the poem, and man not unlike the "undefeatable" animal in the fable, whether the huge opponent has been monstrous beasts, natural calamities, oppressive rulers, or even some less visible enemy. The least visible, of course, may be the worst of all, and Muir's poetry shows, for all his "gentleness" which critics have perhaps stressed too much, great awareness of the latent cruelties and inexplicable attacks that life—and man, and Muir himself—seem to guard as scourges of pride and assurance. One short poem gives forcible expression to this, "The Face":

> See me with all the terrors on my roads,
> The crusted shipwrecks rotting in my seas,
> And the untroubled oval of my face
> That alters idly with the moonlike modes
> And is unfathomably framed to please
> And deck the angular bone with passing grace.
>
> I should have worn a terror-mask, should be
> A sight to frighten hope and faith away,
> Half charnel field, half battle and rutting ground.
> Instead I am a smiling summer sea
> That sleeps while underneath from bound to bound
> The sun- and star-shaped killers gorge and play.

"A sight to frighten hope and faith away". Muir had undoubtedly felt such presences, and his later poetry, some of it on themes of atomic war, is much concerned with it, but he persisted obstinately on his journey ("The heart in its stations / Has need of patience") and was rewarded with those lyrical gleams of quiet meditative joy or hopefulness which are among his most personal utterances—poems like "The Bird" (a beautiful Bridges-like counter-poem to "The Face"), "The Question", "A Birthday", "In Love for Long", "The Debtor", "The Poet", and "I have been taught by dreams and fantasies". The particular sweetness of Muir's lyrical style when it is successful is like the sudden scent of some wild flower which a freer inspiration has allowed to break through the rather abstract and heraldic character of his verse, as, for instance, in "A Birthday":

> I never felt so much
> Since I have felt at all
> The tingling smell and touch
> Of dogrose and sweet briar,
> Nettles against the wall,
> All sours and sweets that grow
> Together or apart
> Together or apart
> In hedge or marsh or ditch.
> I gather to my heart
> Beast, insect, flower, earth, water, fire,
> In absolute desire,
> As fifty years ago.

The group of brooding prophetic reflections on future war and destruction which he wrote in the 1950s—"The Horses", "After a Hypothetical War", "The Last War", "Petrol Shortage", "The Day Before the Last Day"—is a powerful though imperfect last attempt by Muir to speak more directly than through myth and symbol on issues that haunted and distressed him. Perhaps because he is looking forward —however doubtfully—instead of back, perhaps because in these poems the air of science-fiction lends paradoxically a greater reality and urgency than is usual with Muir, this group of poems leaves a strong impression (a much stronger impression, for example, than the poems on specifically Christian themes which he was also developing in the 1950s).

> The sun rises above the sea, and they look and think:
> "We shall not watch its setting." And all get up
> And stare at the sun. But they hear no great voice crying:
> "There shall be no more time, nor death, nor change,
> Nor fear, nor hope, nor longing, nor offence,
> Nor need, nor shame." But all are silent, thinking:
> "Choose! Choose again, you who have chosen this!
> Too late! Too late!"
> And then: "Where and by whom shall we be remembered?"

These poems form, as he says, an "imaginary picture of a stationary fear", the fear that a possible atomic devastation would destroy not only what is physical but human values as well ("No place at all for bravery in that war"). Yet by a curious closing of the circle he brings this fear round to his own intimations of hope, by suggesting in "The Horses" and "Petrol Shortage" that a post-devastational return to primitive pastoral life might restore man to the protection of the earth he had become increasingly estranged from. Men who have no tractors begin to tame wild horses:

> Our life is changed; their coming our beginning.

Butter describes this as "a vision of a more hopeful kind" and also quotes John Holloway's statement that though in Muir's vision "the powers of evil were great, ultimately the powers of good and goodness were greater; and they were greater because they were also humbler, more primaeval, nearer to life in its archaic simplicity". Well, one man's hope is perhaps another man's despair. Muir's primitivism, returning all post-atomic mankind to an Orkney farm, not without a certain austere satisfaction, seems to me to be more insulting than comforting to man's restless spirit and aspiring brain. Let your survivors tame the horses of the Moon, the dragons of Mars: I would call that hope. But Muir was in search of a simplicity which the future was unlikely to reveal unless by a return to the past, and even the simplicity of the past is more myth than reality. So weakness mingles with strength in his search: the weakness of an underlying evasion and escape, the strength of a sincere and moving desire for good. Muir retreats from the wonderful challenge which the apparent menace of the scientific and political future has thrown down to us in mid-century, but he expresses the menace in unforgettable images:

> I see the image of a naked man,
> He stoops and picks a smooth stone from the ground,
> Turns round and in a wide arc flings it backward
> Towards the beginning. What will catch it,
> Hand, or paw, or gullet of sea-monster?
> He stoops again, turns round and flings a stone
> Straight on before him. I listen for its fall,
> And hear a ringing on some hidden place
> As if against the wall of an iron tower.

COLIN FALCK

WILLIAM EMPSON

Seventeenth century philosophy was dominated by rationalist meta-physics, the vision of an eternal reality completely accessible to human reason. This idea, which on the continent gave way to the Kantian dualism of empirical reality and creative spirit (the philosophical root of the Romantic movement) and to the historical and aesthetic philo-sophy of Hegel, lingered on in this country right down to the Cam-bridge of the 1920s. It emerged here in the theory of language of Wittgenstein's *Tractatus Logico-Philosophicus*, whereby propositions "picture" facts and the true propositions of language mirror reality as a whole. It yielded, finally, through its own inconsistencies and the attacks of logical positivism, to the later theory of Wittgenstein's *Philosophical Investigations*, where language no longer stands apart from the world but falls into place as a part of it, as a range of activities in which certain members of that world engage.

Neither of Wittgenstein's theories leaves much room for poetry or the imagination. The *Tractatus* theory, seeing all language as descriptive, leads to "the inexpressible" and to the theory of the pseudo-statement; the *Investigations* theory, treating language as mere activity, ignores the whole rationale of its change and development. With philosophy in this state, our best modern poetics has in fact been a series of attempts to rationalise and domesticate the Romantic-Symbolist tradition. The starting point has been the Coleridgean theory of the imagination, which (heavily based on the German Romantics) was an attack on the idea of a neutral public world governed by reason and immune in principle from the vicissitudes of private emotion: the imagination is seen as a recreating lyrical centre through which external reality is re-invested with emotion and so with human meaning. On this view the poem comes to be a single unique whole, or (in the Hegelian phrase of some recent critics) a concrete universal, and therefore essentially beyond paraphrase. Here the gulf between Image and discourse yawns; and with the sudden vision of one lyrical moment recreating the entire universe this has seemed to lead either to Mallarmé's doctrine of the poem as a pure non-discursive thing or else to the feared *dérèglement* of Rimbaud. For the most part common-sense has intervened; but questions like what counts as a single poem, what is the relation between symbol and statement, and what are the limits of paraphrase continue to nag at us today.

Progress could be made with the help of a better theory of language, and something of the kind is now perhaps available. Pure Imagist theory, the aspiration to the condition of music and the generial irrationalist tendency in the Romantic tradition (the Eugene Jolas Manifesto is a good modern version) all come from the need to defend art against rationalist thinking. On a theory like that of Wittgenstein's *Tractatus*, for example, there is nothing distinctive for a poem to do: reality is what it is, and language describes it; poetry is either part of that language, indistinguishable from other kinds of describing, or else it makes no statements at all and must elude reason entirely. But the rationalist approach can now be rejected, and recent philosophy in this country, using arguments drawn from Kant and Hegel, has at last carried this rejection through decisively. The *Tractatus* theory fails in the end by leaving no room for differences of personal standpoint and concrete context, and so giving no adequate account of the way we experience ourselves and other people within the world that language is supposed to describe. The objections to Wittgenstein's later theory are of an almost opposite kind: over-reacting against the descriptive idea, this view of language as mere activity excludes the whole referential dimension from the start, and with it, therefore, the question of whether or not our language is adequate to the world we use it in. Both of Wittgenstein's theories are magnificent half-truths which have generated our most important modern philosophy between them. But a coherent account of language must see it under both aspects, as vision of the world and as human behaviour. And then it becomes clear that the only possible philosophical picture is of separate and unique individuals living in a single world and continually developing their language through the use of old words in new concrete situations. Which is to say that the organic principle of all language is metaphor.

This means that where poetry is concerned the Coleridgean theory of the imagination is not just a literary fashion but more like a philosophical truth. And this conception of language has direct implications for poetry in so far as it undermines some of the more troublesome distinctions that have been drawn between poetry and prose. The poem is part of the *res*, but it is also about it; and conversely, a prose statement is also a thing. The poem may be strictly unparaphraseable, but so, strictly, is any statement outside the formal systems of logic and mathematics (which of course dominated Cambridge philosophy in the early part of this century); paraphraseability is a matter of degree and convenience. "Pure" poetry therefore has the ground cut from under it: discourse and Image are reconciled in the definition not only of poetry but of language itself, and the purely practical and purely creative uses of language are limiting cases with no real existence. It requires imagination to learn a language; and even the impersonal systems of science are abstracted from and imaginatively based in personal experience, however much we may come to think of them as standing up in their own right. Poetry must in the end be distinguished and for the most part judged by the depth and range of its personal insight: this is what symbolic structure and unity means, and obviously there are no external rules for the judging. Mallarmé was right to see the poetry-prose distinction in these terms, but finally it is one of degree only. And the approximation of poetry and prose is still limited by the rhythmic and gestural demands made on poetry by its verse lay-out and its closer relation to spoken language; in this it is situated differently from, say, the symbolist novel.

This reconciling of Image with discourse and aestheticism with truth makes greater sense of T. S. Eliot's remark about "a logic of the imagination as well as a logic of concepts", and it makes greater nonsense of the attacks on it by critics like Yvor Winters. Hart Crane said the same thing when he wrote of the poem as giving the reader "a single, new word" and as being "raised on the organic principle of a 'logic of metaphor', which ante-dates our so-called pure logic and which is the genetic basis of all speech, hence consciousness and thought-extension". What is in question is the whole nature of language. In life concepts evolve through exposure to the contingent, and the same must be true in poetry: the poem must create within itself some kind of concrete context, a periphery of denoted things which puts the connotations of certain words under tension. This idea has been well developed by Allen Tate, and it seems to me the main criterion of strength in any poetry; though whether real tension—real imagination —is present can be decided only by an appreciative exegesis of the poem, and it is here that reason "gets at" poetry.* This does not mean that abstractions are barred: relatively they constitute one necessary pole of any poem. But they cannot be the main substance of poetry, and least of all today. (One thinks, perhaps, of Wallace Stevens; but Stevens also deals with the experience of abstracting, and this is one human activity along with the rest.) The circle must open on to the concrete and personal somewhere, and the abstractions be brought under tension and redeemed.

The main insights of the Romantic-Symbolist tradition therefore stand: the imagination as centripetal and open to all experience, the need for a concrete standpoint to attain universality from, and a kind of pragmatic holism (what counts as a unity depends on the perspective you take). With the re-admission of "discourse" they add up to the only theory possible today. But there are special modern conditions as well. The trouble with recent pickings at the idea of "the dissociation of sensibility" is that they leave us wondering if there is really no difference at all between the twentieth century and the seventeenth or even the twelfth, and this is obviously absurd. The short truth is that along with theory the world itself has changed: Romanticism was also a movement which arose in particular historical conditions. The essence of romantic, or existentialist, theory is the recognition of the ultimate subjectivity of all our beliefs. But the acceptance of this theory is a historical fact, and it is this acceptance which has virtually constituted our whole modern sensibility. The loss of innocence, whatever we call it, is not reversible, and the great systems of belief, mediaeval and seventeenth century alike, have lost their hold on our imagination. Romanticism, like all theories about ourselves, is perhaps partly self-confirming: we make pictures of ourselves and then come to resemble them, and it may be pointless to ask whether Romanticism just discovered the breakdown of belief or actually constituted it. One real factor is certainly the growing domination of life by the practical world

---

* *Since writing this I have come to be more doubtful about exegesis. Whether real imagination is present, I should now say, can be decided only by the intuition of the really imaginative reader. Exegesis sometimes helps.*

of science. Either way the breakdown is there, and it is the essential difference between the twentieth century and the seventeenth. "Metaphysical" poetry (however accidentally it came by its name) rests on a belief in the possibility of deductive metaphysics; this belief was false, but it lay at the heart of the seventeenth century sensibility. Today, on the other hand, we can no longer detach our beliefs from their point of origin in our own lives, and our only absolute is in fact in the deepest awareness of this relativity. The philosopher has become first and foremost a phenomenologist, and in poetry we must deal not only with our experience but with our whole way of experiencing: honesty demands that the poet should in some way be present in his poems. This is the first insight of Romanticism: we are led to believe in a lie when we see with, not through, the eye. Poetry therefore comes to be the source and continuous re-creation of our morality and understanding, and to the degree that it regenerates our beliefs it cannot presuppose them. Metaphysical poetry is now impossible, and the poetry of intellectual statement must seem empty without some personal centre through which the ideas are re-created. Allen Tate, contrasting the metaphysical and the romantic as extremes of poetic strategy, has written that

> The metaphysical poet, as a rationalist, begins at or near the extensive or denoting end of the line; the romantic or Symbolist poet at the other, intensive end; and each by a straining feat of the imagination tries to push his meanings as far as he can towards the opposite end, so as to occupy the entire scale.

(The extension of a term, here as in strict logic, is the range of objects it denotes; its intension is what it connotes, its verbal implications.) This brings out the metaphysical poet's way of starting with an idea and carrying its analysis through a range of denoted things with no special regard for the implications and resonances of the things themselves. The same ideal of analysis and of a purely extensional language underlies the Cambridge philosophy of the *Tractatus* period. But Tate also implies that the metaphysical and romantic strategies are equally available at any time, and this cannot be right. Given a general faith in systems (though not, the very act of writing poetry suggests, in any particular one), the seventeenth century poet can work confidently by reason and argument; the conceit is the natural expression of this sensibility. But today the systems are shattered and their fragments crumbled into the modern waste land: we have to imagine what we know, and the ideas must be proved upon our pulses. This means that the pressure is now towards the romantic end of the scale, towards awareness of and development through the connotations of words in all their directions: we can no longer keep reality at arm's length with ideas but must work on the words themselves with our bare hands. The modern poem is a part, or perhaps an aspect, of the unique configuration of the poet's mind; and this is a matter of logic, not psychology. Modern poetry is a lyricism of total experience, whatever scale it is on, and is severed from all belief *qua* belief; which is not to say that moral beliefs may not play a large part in our way of experiencing things. (T. S. Eliot, the critic most responsible for the metaphysical revival, seems to be in the romantic line as a poet, in so far as he combines a wide modern intellect with an intense personal lyricism.) What we cannot do today is follow the intellectual path that the poet shows us and be willing to exclude whole ranges of meaning which are not meant to be relevant. In his "Tension in Poetry" essay Tate offers these lines from Cowley:

> The Violet, springs little Infant, stands,
> Girt in thy purple Swadling-bands

and points out that they are absurd because the poet concentrates on analysing the *idea* of infancy and remains oblivious to the surrounding connotations of the swaddling-bands. This is true; and yet they might have seemed less absurd in the seventeenth century, and poets like Cowley and Cleveland might have been less impressed by some of our objections than we are now. The threshold of the grotesque is surely lower today than at any time in the past. Our natural reaction to analysis, however ingeniously pursued, is one of impatience, and we beat off down the side-tracks of connotation that the poet did not mean us to take: we feel all round the individual words. With the greatest poetry this was always possible and added to the achievement: the more side-tracks that could be followed, the better the poem. But today the paths are grown over and ordinary achievement seems to be more a matter of exploring an area in a continually changing jungle.

I have gone on at this length because I could see no way of talking about Mr. Empson's poetry without first making some general prejudices clear. But if justification is really needed there may be enough in the fact that Empson, as well as displaying qualities of mind not easily understood in terms of poetry alone, has rightly or wrongly been seen as a major influence behind the style of poetry which dominated the last decade and which is now overdue for assessment by some serious critical standards.

The most striking thing about Empson's earlier poems is their stylistic assurance and the sense of intellectual excitement they carry: the excitement is part of the whole intellectual atmosphere of Cambridge at that time. Using wide ranges of modern ideas, many of them taken from science, these poems work by argument and conceit with the control and relentlessness of metaphysical poetry at its best. This kind of poetry will often be difficult, not least where the ideas themselves are difficult; and Empson occasionally lets a poem develop through a mass of conflicting metaphors and clang-associations until the result cannot be read without continual reference to the Notes. This tendency is always present, but there are many poems where the obscurity comes a long way short of this, and in "To an Old Lady", which has been called Empson's best poem, there is a spaciousness and clarity which is unusual:

> Ripeness is all; her in her cooling planet
> Revere; do not presume to think her wasted.
> Project her no projectile, plan nor man it;
> Gods cool in turn, by the sun long outlasted.
>
> Our earth alone given no name of god
> Gives, too, no hold for such a leap to aid her;
> Landing, you break some palace and seem odd;
> Bees sting their need, the keeper's queen invader.
>
> No, to your telescope; spy out the land;
> Watch while her ritual is still to see,
> Still stand her temples emptying in the sand
> Whose waves o'erthrew their crumbled tracery.
>
> Still stand uncalled-on her soul's appanage;
> Much social detail whose successor fades,
> Wit used to run a house and to play Bridge,
> And tragic fervour, to dismiss her maids.

Years her precession do not throw from gear.
She reads a compass certain of her pole;
Confident, finds no confines on her sphere,
Whose failing crops are in her sole control.

Stars how much further from me fill my night.
Strange that she too should be inaccessible,
Who shares my sun. He curtains her from sight,
And but in darkness is she visible.

The poem comes over at first or second reading with only slight help from the Notes, and, though not quite typical, it is a good poem through which to see the early Empsonian manner. Despite its subject it is not really personal: as A. Alvarez has pointed out, Empson is related less closely to Donne than to the later Metaphysicals. What it has is the driving assurance of the metaphysical style, which here runs through a handful of ideas (in this case not specially modern) and a range of expression from the Elizabethan to the modern off-hand and somehow manages to seem dignified and convincing in its overall effect.

I want to suggest, all the same, that this poem is fundamentally grotesque. I think its effectiveness depends on our being able to transfer to it our whole quality of response to the metaphysical poetry of the past while taking in at the same time certain modern facts, ideas and turns of phrase. Perhaps it is not surprising if we can almost do this: after all, there has not really been enough modern poetry of this kind to confuse our traditional responses. We have had a few ironical exercises from Eliot, and then almost nothing until the pastiches of, say, Richard Wilbur. The difference with "To an Old Lady" is that a visibly modern subject is being approached with immense underlying seriousness; and I think this modernness and intensity in the poem's subject is sufficient alone to break the spell of its outward manner. When this actually happens, the more metaphysical of the individual lines stand out as potentially ludicrous and the poem's component styles fall apart in all their incongruity. Looked at without prejudice, the association of the old lady with the projectile is rich in undignified possibilities. So, for that matter, is the telescopic watching of her ritual. "Gods cool in turn" has all-too-human implications which the poem would be better without. "Precession" is meant to suggest the dignity of "procession", but to some people it could suggest the relative

C

indignity of, say, bicycle wheels; in fact there is too much machinery around altogether. And once these embarrassing connotations have crowded in and shattered the metaphysical framework it becomes absurd that lines like "Landing, you break some palace and seem odd" should co-exist in the same poem with lines like "Whose waves o'erthrew their crumbled tracery".

It may be said that one should not look for these embarrassing meanings. But the answer is that one does not have to look for them: they are there, and in a modern poem it is impossible to bracket them off. With most of the other early poems, of course, there is not really a spell to be broken in the first place. We have to accept a poem like "Bacchus" on Empson's own terms or not at all: we read it for the argument (and in "Bacchus" the argument throws a good deal of light on Empson's problems). The impression that "To an Old Lady" makes, on the other hand, is not obtrusively intellectual, and it is only because it is potentially moving in a direct way and has a real old lady in it somewhere that it can be, given its general style, absurd. When Empson himself deflates the grand manner, as in "Note On Local Flora" (though deflating is not the main intention, I am sure), it is impossible not to look back and wonder about "To an Old Lady".

It seems to me, then, that this kind of poetry demands in the reader a general obliviousness to the connotations of things which is quite remote from the modern sensibility. Other lines which strike me as regrettable, for all the ingenuity of the poems they come from, are:

> But oh beware, whose vain
> Hydroptic soap my meagre water saves

or

> From infant screams the eyes' blood-gorged veins
> Called ringed orbiculars to guard their balls;

but the point is not so much in particular lines as in the general manner. In "To an Old Lady" or "Arachne" there is a fairly well pruned argument, whereas with "Sea Voyage", "High Dive" or "Bacchus" the poems ramify a great deal more. The difference is really one of degree though, and the essential method is the hyper-metaphysical one of bringing things into the poem and using only a glancing minimum of their meaning to build the argument. For the rest, the things relate only in the poet's mind; and this, as with a crossword puzzle, is not itself present, so that the effect in the end is very often of a kind of surrealism of the intellect. The poetry is centrifugal in tendency, erupting in individual strong lines; and since the connotations of things are over-ridden, no words are brought under pressure or re-created. The poems are festooned from various ideas and abstractions outside, and the greater part of the operative meaning of each thought has no resonance elsewhere in the poem: there is consequently no imaginative centre of any structure except one of argument. This general arrogance towards connotation is shown in a violent ellipsis like "Bees sting their need"; and in the combined ellipsis and circumlocution of—from a later poem—"Who call no die a god for a good throw" (the *idea* is surely very simple?) the arrogance is linked to awkwardness in a more truly Empsonian way. The real intensity of lines like "Poise of my hands reminded me of yours" comes, in fact, from their outward ungainliness and paralysed feel. And this commitment to the extreme metaphysical technique means, finally, that even in the clearer poems the things discussed will exert very little pull back on the poem's argument. At the end of "This Last Pain" there is a long and impressive conceit, and many of the lines are individually powerful, but this does not alter the fact that the poem as a whole rests on an abstract proposition ("Feign then what's by a decent tact believed") and that you tend to settle for it by whether or not you agree. ("Man, as the prying housemaid of the soul" is disturbing in several ways too.) As to agreement, it seems to me that many of these earlier poems deal with personal problems in a way that shows a good deal of moral awareness; but I think one must take care not to confuse questions of this kind with questions of poetic value, and I have not been concerned here with what the poems actually say.

The difference in Empson's later poems is that the moral awareness has undermined the whole earlier manner. As A. Alvarez has shown, the logical drive of the early poems gives way to a static quality and there is a general shift from metaphysical development towards single-line propositions and refrains. Consider these lines from "Aubade":

> It seemed the best thing to be up and go.
> Up was the heartening and the strong reply.
> The heart of standing is we cannot fly.

or from "Missing Dates":

> It is the poems you have lost, the ills
> From missing dates, at which the heart expires.
> Slowly the poison the whole bloodstream fills.
> The waste remains, the waste remains and kills.

What has come to the front here, it seems to me, is a deep awareness of the inadequacy of intellectual modes of comprehension for wresting order from the personal chaos. It is as though Empson had now seen the bankruptcy of the metaphysical technique, but instead of allowing the intellect to collapse decided to shore it up, as another way of saying the same thing. We need beliefs to live, but in affirming this need the new style at the same time suggests a sharp fear of their emptiness. These bare propositions, shorn of metaphor, we feel, cannot really be meant to convince on the deepest level: like proverbs they fit everything, and their opposites are always available. And yet they remain somehow illuminating. It is this, I think, which gives some of these later poems their pathos, with the sense they convey of the whole rationalist intellect falling apart. Their appalling objectivity shows the search for propositions to handle experience with carried to some kind of stunned limit; and this is, of course, reinforced by the metrics and rhyming, which give some of the lines the numbed quality of statements beyond all feeling. A poem like "Missing Dates" seems in the end, to take a phrase from Wittgenstein, like someone trying to mend a spider's web with his fingers. Once we are no longer led on by the metaphysical intellect the central blankness comes to seem colossal and oppressive, so that in a strange way the poet is now almost present in his poems and visible through the gaps between the propositions. What this recalls most of all, perhaps, is Wittgenstein's remarks at the end of the *Tractatus*, which amount to his recognition of the final inadequacy of rationalism and of all that he had said before:

> My propositions are elucidatory in this way: he who understands me finally recognises them as senseless, when he has climbed out through them, on them, over them. (He must so to speak throw away the ladder, after he has climbed up on it.)
> He must surmount these propositions; then he sees the world rightly.

Which of course does not mean that any other propositions would have done just as well.

But if the later poems are in this way more personal they remain static, and they are not personal as poetry is: the emotions felt are precisely not expressed in any personal vision of the outside world. Instead, what is shown by poems like "Aubade" or "Missing Dates" comes to be said explicitly, as in "Let it go":

> It is this deep blankness is the real thing strange.
> The more things happen to you the more you can't
> Tell or remember even what they were.

> The contradictions cover such a range.
> The talk would talk and go so far aslant.
> You don't want madhouse and the whole thing there.

One can see that even to say this would help a bit. The poem, as I see it, is really about the whole business of using general propositions to understand one's experience. And in being about this it is at the same time about not submitting to experience in its totality, with all the possibilities of derangement that might be involved. Like psychology, this is the intellect turned inwards, the self looking at the self. "Let it go", it seems to me, states the central problem and illuminates the other poems in a terrifying way. What we have to ask is: could we imagine a romantic poet trying to "tell or remember even" what had happened to him? It might seem that the answer is yes, and that this goes more for the romantic poet than any other. But I think this would be wrong; what the romantic poet attempts to do is not so much to "tell or remember" what has happened to him as to convert it into poetry. He is interested not in memory but in imagination. It is not so much that the contradictions cover such a range as that the whole problem is to know what terms to use; and the intellect here can only take us to the starting-line. If we read "Let it go" as some kind of realisation of this it takes on an unnerving kind of power, because it means "You cannot do this whole thing with the intellect." A line like "The contradictions cover such a range" comes to seem an almost unbearably painful insight, because it sums up the choice between the intellect and poetry. By rationalist thinking, propositions which conflict cannot both be true, and if we try to handle our experience with them we shall live in permanent contradiction: this is the price of all irritable reaching after fact and reason. But by the kind of logic on which romanticism and any poetry depend the contradictions may be reconcilable on some other level through taking in the outside world with the imagination and bodying the emotions forth in poetry. This is not to advocate going mad; the last irony of this poem, I think, is that it is only through the things that happen to us that we can find out whether reliance on the intellect or on the imagination is most likely to lead to the madhouse. The romantic begins from his own unique bodily situation in the world, and in an insane world this can mean insanity; the intellect must work with what R. D. Laing has called the "unembodied self", and this means a sensibility dissociated from the start.

The awareness of the destructive element is never far away in Empson's later poems, and it is this which makes their blankness so compelling. But in "Ignorance of Death" or "Courage means Running", which seem to me the most impressive from this point of view, there is a certain kind of calm and moral lucidity; and there is an increasingly open style which becomes almost conversational in "Autumn on Nan-Yueh". I think one ought to call this wisdom, but whatever it is it goes with the wry humour and the Johnsonian realism in some of the early poems and with the sustained courageousness of all the poems over things like religion and personal responsibility. Empson's participation in the intellectual brilliance of Cambridge seems to have gone along with a sense of certain deeper inadequacies. The early poems like the early criticism, seem directed at an ideally intelligent audience which existed nowhere in reality, but in his later writing the tone has changed. There is some way in which Empson is deeply English, despite the whole abstract cast of his work; and because of this Englishness his confrontations with other cultures and attempts to assimilate them are strangely impressive.

But this moral wisdom rests, I am suggesting, on a refusal of poetry, and it seems to me that we have to make our choice. Empson has more or less endorsed this himself by saying that all modern poetry seems to be in the Imagist tradition and that no one seems interested in conflict any more. For myself I wish this were more true, but what is clear is that Empson has reached the opposite conclusion and committed himself to a certain kind of poetry of moral statement. One of the most moving things, looking at his poetry as a whole, is the way the translations from Miss Hatakeyama, and especially "The Small Bird to the Big", stand there as a kind of permanently unheeded reminder. Because Empson has rejected Imagism, I cannot in the end like what he has done. It seems to me that the Imagist ideals (essentially there in Coleridge for that matter) of concentration, clear imagery, live rhythms, natural language and a complete openness of subject-matter are absolute requirements for poetry today. In practice Empson has denied almost all of these, along with the further need for the modern poet to be in some way present at the centre of his poem. The Empsonian diction and metrics are a remarkable and unique solution to the form and content problem, but the solution is an authoritarian one: this way of allowing the poem's outward scheme to dictate its inner content leads to a rhetoric in the teeth of natural meaning which is at some kind of opposite pole from poetry. Which is not to say that general propositions are ruled out, but only to demand that they should be in some way concretely re-created: we cannot afford to be weary of the visible. It is because the refrains in "Aubade" hinge on some real situation that I find this the best of Empson's poems in the end. On the other hand, the early "Note on Local Flora" is impressive in a different way and attains a kind of Imagist intensity through its final line and through being formally less mechanical than usual.

Romantic poetry is a taste in the head; but it is also about the world in its entirety. The only method I can see for poetry now is in an openness to words themselves and an ability to see through and not with the eye: we must work outwards towards ideas and not inwards from them. And this is not to insist on any one style alone. But what Empson has done is in its own way heroic; it is a kind of Götterdäm- merung of the rationalist intellect, and it is unrepeatable. For this reason the attempt to do the same kind of thing in the nineteen-fifties could never have led anywhere. Empson's poetry, as one critic said of Wittgenstein's philosophy, is like an arrow which points so unerringly in the wrong direction that by following it the opposite way you nearly always arrive at some valuable truth. What I have said will no doubt seem nagging and ungrateful; but I find it hard to get some of these lines out of my head, and I hope Empson will go on and write some more one day, because no one else can.

the Review No. 6/7

GABRIEL PEARSON

YVOR WINTERS

In most contemporary critical vocabularies the word "restraint" is rarely used pejoratively, and "exuberance" and "excess" rarely as recommendation: this betrays how secretly potent nostalgia for the certitude of neo-classical canons is today. "Restraint" implies praise not only for the discretion and appropriateness with which content is handled, but also for a certain quality of the work, or distinction of mind behind it. If anyone could be found to praise Yvor Winters's *Collected Poems*, "restraint" would doubtless figure among the terms of applause. Here, "restraint" would stand in contrast to the abandon of romantic egoism and expressionism. It wouldn't be that Winters had much to restrain. Simply that he was, his poems were, restrained.

The poems are angled to hook such judgements. Winters slips obtrusively out of his poems, holds up their husks to show how courageously, how unromantically, he has vacated them. That, of course, is occupation at second remove. It would be simply sly, without the presence of that other prime ingredient of neo-classical romantic recoil: nostalgia for an impossible rectitude, some simple ladder of ascent to a deity that has established it precisely to be scaled by consciousness. Winters doesn't just want to imply presence through absence (having his ego and eating it) but, more affectingly, to abolish the situation which compels such ruses. One way out is not just to affect simple-mindedness, but actually to be simple-minded. This works well for opinions, which can suffer almost endless contraction into stereotype. The medium of verse, however, betrays more double-play than Winters wants to appear:

> The State is voiceless: only, we may write
> Singly our thanks for service past, and praise
> The man whose purpose and remorseless sight
> Pursued corruption for its evil ways.

This, from a sonnet "On The Death of Senator Thomas J. Walsh", is, on the face of it, willed shoddiness. "Sight" can hardly be remorseless

(Winters elsewhere shows too much competence to be fatally compelled by rhyme), while the last line, besides looking tautological, pretends absurdly that corruption could be imagined having "good ways". (Renaissance allegorists avoid this kind of muddle by actually embodying the terms of their allegory.) Being clever at Winters's expense is too easy game; besides, he is rarely as bad as this. Interest lies, to employ against him one of Winters's own favourite terms, in the motive. This declares itself around the carefully stationed word "singly". The sonnet opens:

> An old man more is gathered to the great,
> Singly, for conscience' sake he bent his brow. . . .

Winters, through his poem, connects Walsh's single-minded and lonely self-dedication (allowing that these existed) with the poet's own lonely self-dedication to his craft. There is nothing wrong with this way of prasising your own activity under guise of praising someone else's. The repetition of "singly" allows everything about Walsh to be felt about the poet. The reader is drawn into complicity with a select band who bend their brows "for conscience' sake". And that too is a common enough trick of rhetoric. Odder, though, is the way that the badness of the poem—the laboured terms of praise, the archaic diction, the clumsily sepulchral gesture—are recommended as distinction, a moral quality of stoic resistance to the corruption of the age. The poem says in effect that you have to be as dead as this, if you are not to be corrupt. This, I think, is the way in which a lot of romantic neo-classical poetry works. Wordsworth's "Ode to Duty" and Arnold's "Merope" are early examples. It is a complicated form of bad faith. Frigidity, conventional cliche, simple- (or single-) mindedness are offered as escape from the deliquescence, outrageousness and complexity of romantic self-discovery. Here the quality of the poem becomes the subject of itself. In the process it is subtly calculated to imply the excellence of the artist in so deftly mounting such bad pastiche. The poet stands outside his own poem. The poem itself is a dead thing, a monument to the spirit that has abandoned it. This confirms the existence of spirit. A deeper motive now becomes apparent. Empson has described this beautifully in his lines about death:

> It is the trigger of the literary man's biggest gun,
> And we are glad to equate it with any achieved calm.

c*

Winters is a literary man to the eyebrows (and there's unease enough lurking under Empson's urbanity as to what he thinks *he* is: though concentric rings of irony pack to the opacity of an authentic presence in tension with, not evading, his situation). Death is indeed the trigger of Winters's biggest gun, and any achieved calm—at no matter what cost in the way of badness—will do to bring to a decent end his game of hide-and-seek with himself. The sonnet's octave begins: "How sleep the great, the gentle and the wise", all of which Winters wants us directly to think him—and how they sleep, indeed! It concludes that they are all

> Dwellers amid a peace that few surmise,
> Masters of quiet among all the dead.

Peace and quiet are what Winters's poems seem mostly to want. A sizeable proportion swoon deathwards with every appearance of complacency. The prevailing tone of the collection is indeed elegiac— elegies sung over himself and the situations with which he has failed to cope and opted out of. Here then is one prime motive. Deathful repose is evoked both to excuse the badness of the poems and to evade responsibility for exploring the limits of the bad faith that produces them. Such exploration, Winters seems to fear, would involve immersion in the secular world. He might drown in it. Death by petrification—a more prolonged, more disguisable and hence preferred suicide—is chosen. Winters tells us that "The poet's only bliss / Is in cold certitude". A convicted man is "locked in stone" while he waits for the state to kill him. Winters expects our machine civilisation "To leave but Cretan myths, a sandy trace / Through the last stone age . . ." The moon is both "Goddess of poetry" and "Maiden of icy stone". These are products of a very cursory spot-check. Death by drowning, in Winters's secret mythology, represents the fate of the modern poet who abandons himself to the flux of experience. The prime example is Crane. Better dry and petrify in the desert than dissipate and dissolve like Crane:

> In the shining desert still
> We must bend us to our will.
> Crane is dead at sea. . . .

Winters knew Crane personally, and his essay on his former friend rather honestly records Winters's ambivalence of repulsion and attraction to what he regards as Crane's deliberate self-abandonment to the

American daemon of utopianism and self-exploration whose arch-
embodiment is Whitman. Still more revealing is the memorial poem
to Hart Crane, where Crane appears as Orpheus, blood-stained and
water-logged, whose passion has dissolved into unmeaning:

> Crying loud, the immortal tongue.
> From the empty body wrung,
> Broken in a bloody dream,
> Sang unmeaning down the stream.

This too is ruse. The tongue is tolerable periphrasis for poet or poem.
Yet, despite the mythical transference, what comes across is a broken
body, its tongue actually torn out and bloody; the image is really felt
beneath its thin layer of diction. Through half-suppressed physical
detail, fear of dismemberment and dissolution becomes apparent.

Winters's loco-descriptive verse (here the genre is used as disguise)
habitually presents the sea or any water as a dissolving and eroding
agent attacking dry, firm land. He is good at landscape, because he can
plausibly put his one allegory across while doing a straightforward job
of description. The conclusion of "The Slow Pacific Swell" conveys a
note of barely concealed panic in relation to earlier lines:

> I have lived inland long. The land is numb.
> It stands beneath the feet, but one may come
> Walking securely, till the sea extends
> Its limber margin, and precision ends.

The end of precision betokens some more universal cataclysm:

> The slow pacific swell stirs on the sand,
> Sleeping to sink away, withdrawing land,
> Heaving and wrinkled in the moon, and blind;
> Or gathers seaward, ebbing out of mind.

"Ebbing out of mind" clearly is the same sort of thing as Crane's
"unmeaning song". Mind and security of ground under foot stand in
the same relationship to each other as romantic self-assertion and oceanic
dissolution. This configuration of images is very similar to Arnold's.
Arnold makes use of a more complicated allegory, which allows for
more complicated balances of feeling. Winters's total *oeuvre* looks, in
contrast, like "Dover Beach", endlessly re-annotated and diffused.
Stone stands in poem after poem against the wet. There are, of course,

complications within this simple scheme: for example, a sub-scheme by which stone stands against organic life. This is essentially a distraction. When towards the close of a fine poem, "A View of Pasadena From The Hills", Winters laments that "man-made stone outgrows the living tree", he is ostensibly making Wordsworth noises about the intrusive outrage of urbanisation against nature. But in the light of Winters's basic configuration of imagery, the "man-made stone" seems really to be the poem he is writing. There is a submerged reference to Lot's wife, whose nostalgia for a doomed city turned her into a pillar of salt. The end of this poem supports this reading:

> And at its rising, air is shaken, men
> Are shattered, and the tremour swells again,
> Extending to the naked salty shore,
> Rank with the sea, which crumbles ever more.

Again, "Dover Beach" is recalled ("naked shingles of the world"). There is syntactical hesitation about how actively the sea crumbles, how passively (Pasadena is described as "superb on solid loam") land lets itself be crumbled—a stutter provoked by anxiety about how solid in fact Winters feels his ground to be. Dryness against wetness is played out not only as allegory in landscape but, as with Arnold, allegory in relationship to literary figures of the past. The case of Crane, who stands to Winters much as Clough to Arnold, is the most dramatic example. Here there is terror and evasion of terror through mythological reference and masking diction. His sonnet "To Emily Dickinson" does concentrate his persistent imagery to the point where its compactness feels dramatic:

> Dear Emily, my tears would burn your page,
> But for the fire-dry line that makes them burn.

Here the dry-wet antithesis works into complexity. Emily Dickinson stands as the corrective (fire-dry) to any temptation to dissolve—into tears, sentimentality, actuality. Through her, Winters establishes poignantly the difficulty of his own position, implying, in the octave, real doubt about the viability of his life's project:

> Yours was an empty upland solitude
> Bleached to the powder of a dying name;
> The mind, lost in the world's lost certitude

That faded as the fading footsteps came
To trace an epilogue to words grown odd
In that hard argument that led to God.

The words "empty", "solitude", "bleached", "dying", "lost" (twice) enact the sense of a project terribly misfired. The last line, by contrast, is difficult to read straight. "Hard" is admiring and self-admiring, but the terminus of Emily Dickinson's and Winters's quest is invalidated by the preceding vocabulary of defeat and the social judgement of "odd". "Tracing an epilogue" is Winters's characteristic activity, one way of bringing to a dead halt in fantasy the contemporary situation grown intolerable. The same goes for Arnold, whose neo-classic structures are tombstones on which to inscribe his own defeat, trusting that the marmoreal fixity of the medium will somehow atone to posterity for the meagreness of the message. Winters's is an extreme version, almost a parody of the Arnoldian *rigor mortis*. Like Arnold, but earlier in his career, with little visible sign of struggle, he opts for "the vasty halls of death" rather than brave the treacherous currents of his situation. And so, like Arnold, but less excusably in view of powerful examples of how it can be done, his poems conspicuously fail to absorb, master and utilise the contemporary world. He withdraws from it in favour of the antique gesture. As in "Dover Beach", he stands helplessly by, watching "ignorant armies clash by night". Arnold half-realises, in contrast to the cocky sage of "Culture and Anarchy", that not only are the armies ignorant but he ignorant of them as well. He half-acknow-ledges what he doesn't know. Winters cannot get even this far with the twentieth century. Either its properties obtrude as menace or are pelted as scapegoat. Only in one or two personal pieces like the late "At the San Francisco Airport" does he allow his poem to dwell in the secular world. This failure is, ultimately, failure of understanding. He wills himself not to know his own century. As critic, he flees, rather than resorts, to the English renaissance, to poets apparently secure in what Winters quaintly terms and feels he ought to have to justify his own stance—"a theistic position". This "theistic position" is even less elaborated in his critical corpus than it is in Arnold's. He seems to need to affirm it as an *a priori* ground for judgement. It stands outside experience, outside even belief. (Winters's poems are in no way religious, though they often imitate religious poetry.) This ground provides, it appears, a useful spot on which to enact his wholesale holocaust of twentieth century reputations—Stevens, Yeats, Eliot, Frost and Crane.

True, this holocaust is a hearty, even cheering blaze. There is something exhilarating about his root-and-branch onslaught, something heroic in his perverse rectitude. It's good (a thoroughgoing Marxist aristotelianism like Lukacs's performs a similar service) for the lit-crit industry to witness reflex idolatries and best-selling lines blasted by prophetic animus. Names too smugly assumed out of reach of judgement in the empyrium, not to say emporium, of exegesis are brutally resubmitted to the flame. In a situation of eclectic conformities, this is an indubitable service. Yet Winters's corpus—both critical and poetic —remains unmistakably a corpse. His neo-classicism, for all its obsessed documentation of the atrocities of two centuries of romanticism, strikes one as a colossal rearguard action leading to inert entrenchment in a wholly defensive posture. However telling his critique of individuals (he's very good, for example, at demonstrating the confusions and contradictions of Eliot's critical positions, without allowing for the way Eliot's poetry requires continual rearrangement of rôles), his total criticism seems simply out of tune with the literature of our times, borne down upon it with the weight of a massive but inapplicable measuring yard. Winters appeared to have recoiled not so as not to plunge and be drowned, but fearing even to be tempted to do so. He has stood outside the world ever since glaring at it rather than repining after it. Arnold's repining indeed makes for the greater plangency of his elegiac note. Not even with the construction of such megaliths as "Merope" and "Balder Dead" did he entirely opt for his own stone-age. Maybe he was just luckier than Winters in possessing more natural talent, the security and connections of a place, however dust-blown a place, in the public world. Even some of the positivism of his country and age naturally rubbed off on him. Winters, however, from the first, sought safety in being simultaneously anterior and posthumous to his age. The blurb refers, it is true, to "an extreme *avant-garde* position" preceding (someone very dead-pan here!) what it calls his "steady regression . . . into an ever more rigorous conservatism". Perhaps, by large-scale omission, Winters has distorted this record of his development. I can discover little that is *avant-garde* in the first twenty-odd poems of the collection save for some spineless and jagged free-verse, some remarkably uncommunicative *haikus* and neo-classical essays in the style of H.D. at her most eviscerated crossed with childhood nostalgias out of Emily Dickinson at her most spiderish. Occasional lines from this period—e.g. "the dogs swim close to earth"—succeed in conveying those tight, inextricable nexuses of sensation that more recent practitioners, such as some of those represented in Donald Hall's anthology, seem good at. But this limited effect crops up in late Winters, firmly buckled indeed into octosyllabic quatrains, to produce some of the best, because least self-assertive, poems (". . . . a dog / Mud-soaked and happy, in a daze / Works into rain as dark as fog"). All the evidence of this volume shows reaction pre-dating any full experience of what was being reacted against. Hence the prevailing narrowness, winteriness and monotony of the poems; hence the premeditated perversity of the critical writings.

The root-motive is still elusive. No doubt it is partly temperamental and personal. Only rarely in the poems is a private life alluded to. There are some fine, though oddly unfeeling lines about his father. Winters is an impersonal poet, not in the sense of being objective, but in there not being much person there. The root-motive can be glimpsed in characteristic pre-occupation, both in his poems and criticism, with pedagogic standards. Unlike European intellectuals, the American artist-intellectual tends to be an academic. He registers the shock of confrontation with his society in the universities. Here he brings the values of his society to the test, decides his options in choice of a life-mode, seeks to determine viable traditions and makes crucial decisions about what should and should not be transmitted. Ezra Pound's *Guide to Kulchur* is very much a product of this. American culture is thought of, like the constitution, as a construct rather than an inheritance. Its values are always to be established, continually demanding re-assessment and refurbishing. This leads both to an endless quest after viable traditions and an attempt to transcend national traditions in favour of a trans-national selection of the best that has been thought and said. Further, American literary studies, on which much of the onus for tradition construction has fallen, have tended to split sharply between a technological accretion of fact (the Germanic tradition of scholarship) and techniques of incisive evaluation (criticism). Add another set of antagonistic drives—one exoteric, making the best that has been thought and said freely available to all; the other esoteric, maintaining the purity of cultural activity against dilution by popular debasement— and the high tension around the pedagogical question becomes maximal. This tension Winters must, with so many others, have been subjected to in the Twenties. He had to settle his standards early if, given his temperamental rigidity, they were not to dissipate in eclecticism, conformity or academic mediocrity. He had likewise to determine his picture of society, its condition, the direction it should take, largely on the basis of its literature. The nation was too complex, dynamic and uncontrolled to penetrate experimentally in any depth, save at immense personal cost. And all this, presumably, upon the instant, faced with the exigencies of how and what to teach. His discussion of the teaching of literature in universities demonstrates the nausea common to responsible academics confronted with the meaningless grind and undirected productivity of the literature industry. He is disgusted by its oppor- tunism, dreads its imposition of mechanistic norms, resists its system of self-boost whereby the contemporary is automatically taken up, ground down small and graded to become grist to its mill. Winters's defensive posture originated, I suspect, as desperate and principled resistance to this machine. The point was, however, what were the principles? Here the long retreat from his own century begins. There were no principles —only warning instincts. So principles had to be fabricated. Winters does not appear to inherit or re-achieve belief in God; he invents, because he feels the need of it, his "theistic position". Rationality is not exercise of one of a spectrum of human faculties, but an esoteric principle, enshrined in extinct systems of belief and their literatures, to be declared, revealed and, above all, defended like a theology against romantic expressionism and utopianism. This process of fabrication in turn assumes its own autonomy, thus reproducing in negative the process it was designed to resist. The affirmations and rejections become more and more wholesale until the bulk of twentieth century literature, of American literature, eventually the whole American experience, is rejected in favour of the life-style, theology and poetics of a number of sixteenth and seventeenth century poets and humanists:

> Gascoigne, Ben Jonson, Greville, Raleigh, Donne,
> Poets, who wrote great poems, one by one.

In its total commitment and manifest implausibility there is—a final irony—something very American and Utopian about this. American cultural self-consciousness seems either local or continental, not national. American Utopianism—and its reverse, daemonism—works not through the grain of grasped national experience, which, as in Britain, necessarily collapses Manichean absolutes, but by reference to archetypes and prototypes employed as ways of understanding society in the absence of more traditional and more plausible models of how it works. Though a lot of nonsense is talked about myths, the American obsession with the mythic element in their own culture is not accidental. These myths are of course factitious, products of literary self-conscious-ness. They are also the way in which the American intellectual instinctively tries to grasp and explain his cultural situation. The paucity of other viable modes—such as would be provided by class, or directly political identity—goes some way to explain this. Even sociological explanations veer towards mythic prototypes of which Burnham's manager and Riesman's other-directed man are recent versions. Winters has reacted apparently in reverse. He has rejected the Whitman-Utopian prototype in the person of Hart Crane. But he has no sympathy either with those modern Bacchae who have mangled Orpheus, who

> ... pause and calculate.
> Then, as such beings use,
> With long-perfected hate,
> Strike the immortal Muse.

Yet Crane, he believes, invited his own nemesis. He abandoned himself wilfully to the forces that cheapen, muddy, commercialise and inject deadly opiates into the stream of American culture. But in rejecting the Crane prototype he has lost vital qualities that go to make a modern poetry: attunement to rhythms of his civilisation, courage to submit to its destructive element, the negative capability to encounter without immediate self-destruction its reality. This has meant also abandoning the pursuit of understanding. Winters's "reason" is the reverse of understanding. It is a defective anti-myth, a desperate dyke improvised in panic against an ocean of unmeaning. Winters's *Collected Poems* reveal how high and dry five decades of this century have left him. His own mythic prototype has become the "masters of quiet" of the

Walsh sonnet, men safely dead, men whose qualities of restraint and singularity his poems can only gesture towards but cannot themselves really demonstrate. This master, this grave humanist, this academic devotee of craft, constructing over long years his precise and logically sustained artifacts, is all that Winters can offer ("now, my only shift") as his positive. And this figure too is nothing but statuary in a fallen world—

> The statue, pure amid the rotting leaves.

a frozen affirmation that stoically endures a final, weary doubt:

> And art endures, or so the masters say.

the Review No. 8

A. ALVAREZ

SYLVIA PLATH

She was a tall, spindly girl with waist-length sandy hair, which she usually wore in a bun, and that curious, advertisement-trained trans-atlantic air of anxious pleasantness. But this was a nervous social manner; under it, she was ruthless about her perceptions, wary and very individual.

She was born in 1932. Her parents were both teachers and both of German origin: her mother Austrian, her father pure Prussian; he died when she was nine. They lived in Boston, Massachusetts: "I went to public school," she wrote, "genuinely public. *Everybody* went." Hers was Wellesley High School. From there she went to Smith College, remorselessly winning all the prizes. In 1955 she got a Fulbright Scholarship to Newnham College, Cambridge. Whilst there she met Ted Hughes, who at that point had published almost nothing, and they were married in 1956. They went to America, where she taught at Smith for a year. In 1959 they returned to England and settled here for good—first in London, then in Devon. By this time she had become a full-time exile. In 1960 her first child, Frieda, was born and her first book, *The Colossus*, was published. Two years later she had a son, Nicholas. In the middle of last January she published her first novel, *The Bell Jar*, using a pseudonym, Victoria Lukas, partly, she told me, because she didn't consider it a serious work—though it was more serious and achieved than she admitted, and got good reviews—and partly because she thought too many people would be hurt by it—which was probably true. She died one month later, on the 11th February, 1963.

Her first poem came out in the *Boston Traveller*, when she was eight-and-a-half. I have no idea what these first poems were like, though their subject matter appears to have been conventional enough. "Birds, bees, spring, fall", she said in an interview,

> —all those subjects which are absolute gifts to the person who doesn't have any interior experiences to write about.

Clearly the poems were very precocious, like everything she did in her school and college days. She seemed effortlessly good at things: she was a prize scholar as well as a prize poet, and later, when she married, she was good at having children and keeping a house clean, cooking, making honey, and even at riding horses. There was a ruthless efficiency in all she did which left no room for mistakes or uncertainties.

Poetry, however, is not made by efficiency—least of all Sylvia Plath's poetry. Instead, her extraordinary general competence was, I think, made necessary by what made her write; an underlying sense of violent unease. It took a great deal of efficiency to cope with that, to keep it in check. And when the efficiency finally failed, her world collapsed.

But she was disciplined in art, as in everything else. For a first volume, by someone still in her twenties, *The Colossus* is exceptionally accomplished. A poem like "The Ghost's Leavetaking" is fairly typical. It exhibits her range of language, in which the unexpected right word comes so easily:

> ... the waking head rubbishes out of the draggled lot
> Of sulphurous landscapes and obscure lunar conundrums

and her ability to make startling images out of humdrum objects:

> The oracular ghost who dwindles on pin-legs
> To a knot of laundry, with a classic bunch of sheets
> Upraised, as a hand, emblematic of farewell.

But that last line is also typical of the book's weakness: it's beautiful all right, but it is also peculiarly careful, held in check, a bit ornate and rhetorical. Throughout *The Colossus* she is using her art to keep the disturbance, out of which she made her verse, at a distance. It is as though she had not yet come to grips with her subject as an artist. She has Style, but not properly her own style. You can trace the influence of Ted Hughes, and there are also poems which sound like Theodore Roethke's—including the long "Poem for a Birthday", which stands last in the book and attempts, I think, to deal with a subject which later possessed her: her nervous breakdown and near suicide at the age of nineteen. It was this which also made the climax and main subject of her novel.

Most of the poems in *The Colossus* were written during the first three years of her marriage, from 1956 to 1959. The *real* poems began in 1960, after the birth of her daughter, Frieda. It is as though the child were a proof of her identity, as though it liberated her into her real self. I think this guess is borne out by the fact that her most creative period followed the birth of her son, two years later. This triggered off an extraordinary outburst: for two or three months, right up to her death, she was writing one, or two, sometimes three, poems a day, seven days a week. She said, in a note written for the B.B.C.:

> These new poems of mine have one thing in common. They were all written at about four in the morning—that still blue, almost eternal hour before cockcrow, before the baby's cry, before the glassy music of the milkman, settling his bottles.

A poem like "Poppies in October" is simpler, much more direct, than those in *The Colossus*. The unexpectedness is still there, both in the language—

> a sky palely and flamily igniting its carbon monoxide

and in the images—

> the woman in the ambulance whose red heart blooms through her coat so astoundingly,

but it is no longer baroque, no longer a gesture on the surface of the poem. It is part of what she is actually saying. The poem is about the unexpectedness of the poppies, their gratuitous beauty in her own frozen life. This change of tone and access of strength is partly, as she said herself, a technical development:

> May I say this: that the ones I've read are very recent, and I have found myself having to read them aloud to myself. Now this is something I didn't do. For example, my first book, *The Colossus*—I can't read any of the poems aloud now. I didn't write them to be read aloud. In fact, they quite privately bore me. Now these very recent ones—I've got to say them. I speak them to myself. Whatever lucidity they may have comes from the fact that I say them aloud.

The difference, in short, is between finger-count and ear-count; one measures the rhythm by rules, the other catches the movement by the inner disturbance it creates. And she could only "write poems out loud" when she had discovered her own speaking voice; that is, her own identity.

The second main difference between this and her earlier verse is in
the direct relevance of the experience. In "The Ghost's Leavetaking"
the subject is nominally very personal—it's about the way dreams stay
with you when you first wake up—but the effect is predominantly of
very brilliant scene-setting. In "Poppies in October", on the other
hand, what starts as a description finishes as a way of defining her own
state of mind. This, I think, is the key to the later poems; the more vivid
and imaginative the details are, the more resolutely she turns them
inwards. The more objective they seem, the more subjective they, in
fact, become. Take, for example, the poem about her favourite horse,
"Ariel". The difficulty with this pem lies in sorting out one element
from another. And yet that is also its theme; the rider is one with the
horse; the horse is one with the furrowed earth, and the dew on the
furrow is one with the rider. The movement of the imagery, like that
of the perceptions, is circular. There is also another peculiarity: although
the poem is nominally about riding a horse, it is curiously "substance-
less"—to use her own word. You are made to *feel* the horse's physical
presence, but not to see it. The detail is all inward. It is as though the
horse itself were an emotional state. So the poem is not about "Ariel",
it is about what happens when the "stasis in darkness" ceases to be
static, when the potential violence of the animal is unleashed. And also
the violence of the rider.

In a way, most of her later poems are about just that: about the
unleashing of power, about tapping the roots of her own inner violence.
There is, of course, nothing so very extraordinary about that. I think
that, in general, this is the direction all the best contemporary poetry is
taking. She, certainly, did not claim to be original in the kind of writing
she was doing:

> I've been very excited by what I feel is the new breakthrough that came
> with, say, Robert Lowell's *Life Studies*. This intense breakthrough into
> very serious, very personal emotional experience, which I feel has been
> partly taboo. Robert Lowell's poems about his experiences in a mental
> hospital, for example, interest me very much. These peculiar private and
> taboo subjects I feel have been explored in recent American poetry—I think
> particularly of the poetess Anne Sexton, who writes about her experiences
> as a mother; as a mother who's had a nervous breakdown, as an extremely
> emotional and feeling young woman. And her poems are wonderfully

craftsmanlike poems, and yet they have a kind of emotional and psychological depth which I think is something perhaps quite new and exciting.

Robert Lowell and Anne Sexton make pretty distinguished company,
but I think Sylvia Plath took further than either of them her analysis of
the intolerable and the "taboo". And she did it in a wholly original
way. For example, her poem, "Fever 103°", which she described in
this way:

> This poem is about two kinds of fire—the fires of hell, which merely
> agonise, and the fires of heaven, which purify. During the poem, the first
> sort of fire suffers itself into the second.

First time through it sounds as though it were just free association on a
theme: the theme that illness and pain are cumbersome and intolerable,
but that if they go on long enough they cancel themselves out and the
purity of death takes over. But the progress is not in fact haphazard.
Death is there from the start: "dull, fat Cerberus ... wheezes at the
gate" right from the beginning. What the poem does is to work away
at this idea of a heavy, mundane death until it is purified of all ex-
traneous matter and only the essential bodilessness remains. At the same
time this movement is also that of a personal catharsis. She is clarifying
not only an abstract death but also her feelings about it, from the clut-
tered and insufferable to the pure and acceptable. Her method is to let
image breed image until, in some curious way, they breed too, statements, conclusions:

> They will not rise,
> But trundle round the globe
> Choking the aged and the meek,
> The weak
>
> Hothouse baby in its crib.
> The ghastly orchid
> Hanging its hanging garden in the air.
>
> Devilish leopard!
> Radiation turned it white
> And killed it in an hour.
>
> Greasing the bodies of adulterers
> Like Hiroshima ash and eating in.
> The sin. The sin.

The baby becomes the orchid, the spotted orchid the leopard, the beast

of prey the adulteress; by which time the fever has become a kind of
atomic radiation (perhaps she was remembering the film *Hiroshima Mon
Amour*). The idea of the individual and the world purged of sin is
established and the poem is free to move on to the realm of purification.
Now, the movement is complicated. Often in these last poems it seems
unnecessarily so. The images came so easily to her that sometimes they
confuse each other until the poems choke in the obscurity of their own
inventiveness. But they never suffer from the final insoluble obscurity
of private references—as, say, Pound's do in the *Pisan Cantos*. The
reasons for Sylvia Plath's images are always there, though sometimes
you have to work hard to find them. She is, in short, always in intelligent control of her feelings. Her work bears out her theories.

> I think my poems come immediately out of the sensuous and emotional
> experiences I have, but I must say I cannot sympathise with these cries from
> the heart that are informed by nothing except a needle or a knife or what-
> ever it is. I believe that one should be able to control and manipulate
> experiences, even the most terrifying—like madness, being tortured, this
> kind of experience—and one should be able to manipulate these experi-
> ences with an informed and intelligent mind. I think that personal ex-
> perience shouldn't be a kind of shut box and mirror-looking narcissistic
> experience. I believe it should be generally relevant, to such things as
> Hiroshima and Dachau, and so on.

It seems to me that it was only by her determination both to face her
most inward and terrifying experiences and to use her intelligence in
doing so—so as not to be overwhelmed by them—that she managed to
write these extraordinary last poems, which are at once deeply autobiographical and detached, generally relevant.

"Lady Lazarus" is a stage further on from "Fever 103°", its subject
is the total purification of achieved death. It is also far more intimately
concerned with the drift of Sylvia Plath's life. The deaths of Lady
Lazarus correspond to her own: the first just after her father died, the
second when she had her nervous breakdown, the third perhaps a
presentiment of the death that was shortly to come. Maybe this closeness of the subject helped make the poem so direct. The details don't
clog each other: they are swept forward by the current of feeling,
marshalled by it and ordered. But what is remarkable about the poem
is the objectivity with which she handles such personal material. She is

clearly more than someone talking about her suffering. Instead, it is the very closeness of her pain which gives it a general meaning. Through it she assumes the suffering of all the modern victims. She becomes the Japanese murdered by the atom bombs. Above all, she becomes an imaginary Jew. I think this is a vitally important element in her work. For two reasons. First because anyone whose subject is suffering has a ready-made modern example of hell on earth in the concentration camps. And what matters in them is not so much the physical torture— since sadism is general and perennial—but the way modern, as it were industrial, techniques can be used to destroy utterly the human identity. Individual suffering can be heroic provided it leaves the person who suffers a sense of his own individuality—provided, that is, there is an illusion of choice remaining to him. But when suffering is mass-produced, men and women become as equal and identity-less as objects on an assembly-line, and nothing remains—certainly no values, no humanity. This anonymity of pain, which makes all dignity impossible, was Sylvia Plath's subject. Second, she seemed convinced, in these last poems, that the root of her suffering was the death of her father, whom she loved, who abandoned her and who dragged her after him into death. And her father was pure German.

It all comes together in the most powerful of her last poems, "Daddy", about which she wrote the following bleak note:

> The poem is spoken by a girl with an Electra complex. Her father died while she thought he was God. Her case is complicated by the fact that her father was also a Nazi and her mother very possibly part Jewish. In the daughter the two strains marry and paralyse each other—she has to act out the awful little allegory before she is free of it.

"Lady Lazarus" ends with a final, defensive, desperate assertion of omnipotence:

> Out of the ash
> I rise with my red hair
> And I eat men like air.

Not even that defence is left her in "Daddy": in it she has gone right down to the deep spring of her sickness and described it purely. What comes through most powerfully, I think, is the terrible unforgiving-ness of her verse, the continual sense not so much of violence—although there is a good deal of that—as of violent resentment that this should have been done to *her*. What she does in the poem is, with a weird detachment, to turn the violence against herself so as to show that she can equal her oppressors with her self-inflicted oppression. And this is the strategy of the concentration camps. When suffering is there whatever you do, by inflicting it upon yourself you achieve your identity, you set yourself free.

Yet the tone of the poem, like its psychological mechanism, is not single and simple. It works on a returning note and rhyme:

> You do not do, you do not do . . .
> . . . I used to pray to recover you.
> Ach, du. . . .

There is a kind of cooing tenderness in this which complicates the other more savage note of resentment. It brings in an element of pity, less for herself and her own suffering than for the person who made her suffer. Despite everything, "Daddy" is a love poem.

When Sylvia Plath died I wrote an epitaph on her in *The Observer*, at the end of which I said "The loss to literature is inestimable". But someone pointed out to me that this wasn't quite true. The achievement of her final style is to make poetry and death inseparable. The one could not exist without the other. And this is right. In a curious way, the poems read as though they were written posthumously. It needed not only great intelligence and insight to handle the material of them, it also took a kind of bravery. Poetry of this order is a murderous art.
the Review No. 9

Note: Since its appearance in *the Review*, this essay has been reprinted in A. Alvarez's collection of essays, *Beyond All This Fiddle* (Allen Lane: The Penguin Press, 1968). Mr. Alvarez has made one or two minor revisions and he has added a Postscript in which he explains that in the final paragraph of his essay he "was *not* in any sense meaning to imply that breakdown or suicide is a validation of what I now call Extremist poetry". Nor was he "in any sense meaning to imply that a breakdown or suicide is the necessary corollary or result of Extremist work". "The very source", he writes, "of (Sylvia Plath's) creative energy was, it turned out, her self-destructiveness. But it was, precisely, a source of *living* energy, of her imaginative, creative power. So, though death itself may have been a side-issue, it was also an unavoidable risk in writing her kind of poem. My own impression of the circumstances surrounding her eventual death is that she gambled, not much caring whether she won or lost; and she lost. Had she won, the power of those last poems would have been in no way altered or falsified, and she would have been free to go on to other work. That she didn't is the real tragedy."

FRANCIS HOPE

THE THIRTIES

Clichés drive out clichés: in the process, we hope, truth is approached. Five or ten years ago it was a commonplace to see the Thirties as the Pink Poet's decade, when some fine talents were marred, and a few ruined, by an extreme concentration on externals dictated by the party line; when an all-pervading concern with politics swept into literature. Today it is becoming a commonplace to see it as the reverse: a period, as Mr. Philip Toynbee wrote, of "intense literary excitement" first and foremost, when an all-pervading concern with literature even swept into politics.

> For the truth is that the "political" thirties were nothing like so heavily political, for the readers of little magazines, as the past ten years have been. Or rather it is fair to say that the politics of middle-class intellectuals in those days were really a kind of hobby—a passionate stimulant rather than a burdensome and cruel necessity. With perfect propriety the poets and novelists of that time took only what they wanted from a political scene which was still remote from them.

Defending themselves against journalistic charges of journalistic practice, the Thirties poets have established how few of their poems were in fact concerned with political subjects; how little of an organised group they actually formed (the Big Four rammed together under Roy Campbell's contemptuous pseudonym Macspaunday were only once, during the whole decade, simultaneously all in the same room); how much the trade of pure literature owes to them. Time, which is indifferent to the Oxford collective poem or *Poems about the Spanish Civil War*, has invested Auden with a retrospective faith and promoted MacNeice for honest doubt. Indeed, the advance of MacNeice's reputation marks the current valuation of the Thirties as surely as mercury in a thermometer: the higher this uncommitted urban lyricist, modern but not contemporary, the further we are from the Left Book Club and the International Brigade. The real Thirties, now, are sought beneath the political surface, in the timeless springs of good writing:

we do not accuse that lost-and-found generation of politicising literature, but of putting too literary a gloss on politics. And out of their own mouths many a middle-aged mellow retrospective glance confirms this diagnosis. Day Lewis's *The Buried Day* is a fine but not a unique example.

Should we take it, and leave it, at this? Surely the Depression and the War, armaments and anti-fascism, China and Spain, have been unburied often enough?

> The Anschluss, Guernica—all the names
> At which those poets thrilled or were afraid
> For me mean schools and schoolmasters and games;
> And in the process something is betrayed.

Separate the poets from the ballyhoo, Auden recently urged on television; judge the tree by its fruits, not by the slogans that someone else has pinned on the orchard. Even if it means accepting those neo-Poundians who dismiss the Thirties as a literary irrelevance (another strong "revisionist" interpretation now going the rounds), shouldn't we keep to the poetical texts?

Certainly some quiet empiricism seems in order. The cross-currents of the period were more complicated than elementary stratifications allow. *New Verse*, for example, published a variety of poets from Dylan Thomas and Philip O'Connor to Norman Cameron and David Gascoyne, as well as Auden, MacNeice, Spender, Allott, Madge, Fuller, Prokosch and Bernard Spencer. It also rarely missed an opportunity to denounce Day Lewis for lickspittle fellow-travelling. (It rarely offered total freedom from denunciation to anybody, which may provide an artificially easy ground for seeing internecine differences.) The personalities of the decade altered their views as the decade wore on: by 1937 Edgell Rickword was upbraiding Auden for having abandoned "that sensuous consciousness of social change which made his early poems such exciting discoveries". Spain quenched almost as much enthusiasm as it kindled; even Baldwin's government either introduced or was blessed by some economic recovery. In Spain itself, as Julian Symons has recorded, the majority of English combatants were workers, not middle-class intellectuals. His book on the Thirties also does the useful service of pointing out how small the numbers actively involved in intellectual life were: Auden's *Poems* sold 3,500 copies in seven years; *The Orators* sold 2,000 in eleven. Respectable, but hardly remarkable. The famous silences of the Forties ("where are the war poets?") marked not only the expiring hopes of a clever, dishonest decade, but a turning away from politics which went deep into the decade's second half. In *Autumn Journal* the spirit of post-war liberalism is already beating strong.

> Nettlebed, Shillingford, Dorchester—each unrolls
> The road to Oxford; *Qu'allais-je faire* tomorrow
> Driving voters to the polls
> In that home of lost illusions?
> And what am I doing it for?
> Mainly for fun, partly for a half-believed in
> Principle, a core
> Of fact in a pulp of verbiage,
> Remembering that this crude and so-called obsolete
> Top-heavy tedious parliamentary system
> Is our only ready weapon to defeat
> The legions' eagles and the lictors' axes. . . .

And as well as empiricism, modesty might temper our hindsight. Once past 1945, Attlee's brand of socialism may seem acceptable and eminently realistic; in 1933 the coming death-agonies of capitalism and social democracy were a more probable bet. We tend to think that because we know that the Great Crash of 1929 was important, we also know what living through it was like, and to measure the intellectual appeal of Marxism by the crudities of the *Daily Worker* or the sibylline obscurities of *New Left Review*. Claud Cockburn, John Strachey and Christopher Caudwell were not fools, and those who were influenced by them can hardly be said to have ignored all the real issues of their time. Early Stalinism was swallowed, the New Deal was wrongly ignored (though not by Cockburn), and books like Geoffrey Gorer's *Nobody Talks Politics* provide rich material for a *sottisier*. All the more credit to people like Orwell or D. W. Brogan, who were isolatedly right. But one cannot dismiss the "left-wing orthodoxy" as a touching blind alley, nor as a marginal interference. It was a more political—or at least a more politically hopeful—period than the present; we enjoy different circumstances, but not necessarily better judgement. Until we outgrow the illusion that the politics can be dismissed we shall not get very far with the poetry; we shall impose our presuppositions on them as surely as they sometimes imposed theirs on history.

It is commonly asserted now (and was then) that as middle-class radicals they failed to connect political ideas with anything that touched them very deeply. Allen Tate, in 1937:

> The well-brought-up young men discovered that people work in factories and mines, and they want to know more about these people. But it seems to me that instead of finding out about them, they write poems calling them Comrades from a distance.

A judgement vindicated by examples too numerous to quote and, in some cases, too obvious to refute. One of the attractions of the Spanish cause may well have been the classlessness which foreigners always miraculously acquire: the embarrassing gulfs between a socialist poet and an English industrial worker were transmuted to a picturesque starkness when the worker was replaced by a Catalan peasant. But one cannot accuse Julian Bell, or Caudwell, or John Cornford of frivolously dabbling in a world to which they had no real commitments. Death in battle is a solider guarantee of sincerity than the most impeccable working-class pedigree. It was political doctrine, rather than social authenticity, that motivated the pre-war left. Today the balance has shifted.

Admittedly, Thirties parties were not free from arguments about whose parents' house had a bathroom, but they tended to be of a rather academic kind. There was proletcult, but few real proletarians: this led to the insincerity Tate deplored, and to such vagaries of bourgeois Marxism as the snobbish assertion that the lower-middle class represented the real scourings of capitalist society; the barrister's son sneered at the clerk's, and called it socialism (Today the lower-middle class has provided far too many of the new intelligentsia for such sentiments to gain wide currency.) But all this didn't occupy quite the front rank that class-obsessed moderns may give it. Some solid political interest and information underlay it—far more, I think, than CND ever dispersed, and CND is the nearest thing to politics that post-war Britain can show. A friend of Spender's once complained to me that he (Spender) had been attacked for crusading in politics without understanding them. "They say that now we have writers like Wesker, who tell us what the working-class is really like, we can see what rubbish Stephen was talking.

And after *Roots*, they still think that Wesker knows about politics. Compare him with Stephen, who really did know—who could tell you what a Viennese Social Democrat was." Between the conception of politics as being in resonance with one's own country's working-class, and the conception of politics as knowing what a Viennese Social Democrat stands for, there is a deep and important gulf. The Thirties' political commitment, like that of well-off English radicals from Byron on, was a European one: and that is now simply unfashionable. We read foreign languages, and travel, less; American academic grants, not the European purchasing power of the pound, are the main prop of the contemporary poet's *wanderjahre*, if he has any. Our horizons are either too small for Europe, or too wide; our own concerns don't straggle beyond Dover and our headlines take in the whole world.

Most literary radicals of the Thirties, I believe, were in a very different situation. For them politics and Europe were almost interchangeable terms. Both were urgent, tragic, and yet liberating areas to explore; fields of great importance, which the old and powerful were too stupid to understand but where the future of civilisation would be settled, and settled soon. Time and again in the poems of the period one finds Europe used as the symbol of political struggle. As Allott wrote:

> From this wet island of birds and chimneys
> who can watch suffering Europe and not be angry?

These Anglo-Eurocentric attitudes may explain their ignorance of American culture as well as American politics. It may also account for the frequent glossing of Soviet crimes as something only to be expected from a primitive, semi-Asiatic nation: Auden (again, on television) ruefully remarked that his contemporaries had felt that the Russians "weren't white folks" and therefore should not be judged too harshly.

If this led them to ignore today's "*supergrands*", it also led them to ignore the Empire. So did anti-patriotism, an emotion for which First World War schooldays must have provided a firm, almost an objective foundation. In one of *Encounter's* interminable symposia on entering the Common Market, Auden wrote:

> Beneath the arguments Pro and Con lie passionate prejudices and the eternal feud between the High-Brow and the Low-Brow. ... I know Europe at first hand, and as a writer I cannot conceive of my life without

the influence of its literature, music and art. The Dominions, on the other
hand, are for me *tiefste Provinz*, places which have produced no art and are
inhabited by the kind of person with whom I have least in common.

For the Low-Brows ... the Dominions are inhabited by their relatives
and people like themselves, speaking English, eating English food, wearing
English clothes and playing English games, whereas "abroad" is inhabited
by immoral strangers—a French novel is synonymous with porno-
graphy ...

A bit quirky? But isn't it also true that one of the great disasters of the
period was that British policy was in the hands of men who really were
more interested in Empire than in Europe, and that they were too old
or too stubborn to change their focus? Ideally an intermediate generation should have forced up a way under them; but nobody, in this
Commemorative Season of 1914, needs to be told where that generation
was. Some arrogant and prickly certainty, some conviction that only
radical change would do, some contemptuous insistence on the war
between young and old, is no more than one would expect from a
generation without elder brothers. Once again their situation was very
different from our own: a mere application of the commonsense of the
Sixties doesn't highlight solutions they were too stupid to see.

The difference cuts both ways, making nonsense of nostalgia as well
as the wisdom of hindsight. As always, the lesson of history is not to
assume lightly that history repeats itself. A return to the spirit of the
Popular Front is not going to revivify either our poetry or our politics.
We know our situation as they knew theirs, and react accordingly; to
revamp an old Thirties slogan—and one that may be quite compatible
with Toynbee's argument—liberalism is the knowledge of impotence.
That superb confidence which is the main virtue of the Thirties poets
was not all of it misplaced confidence. It was in part the inherited moral
capital of a class: of that overlapping ground between the English
gentry and the bourgeoisie which was so supremely sure of its right and
ability to teach, cure, preach to and administer its own inferiors at
home, or whole nations overseas. It was in part the product of a specific
political situation: a country governed by old men, apparently indifferent to the problems to which the poets' inclinations, education,
friendships and knowledge all drove them. It was partly a matter of
individual temperaments: Auden's schoolmasterly certainty combined
with a streak of *enfant-terrible* desire to make the grown-ups' flesh creep

with imaginary horrors (he once told me in conversation that he had always been the youngest child and the youngest grandchild in family gatherings, and still tended to look on himself as the youngest person in any room); or that Wykehamist rectitude that has often infuriatingly protected Labour Party leaders from being irritated by criticism. It did not even survive their own decade. But it was more than an error which time has disproved; more than a passing eccentricity which we luckily will not have to go through, and which we can ignore in our comments on them. It is not a question of what "real poetry" we can salvage from the wreck of convictions, but of hiving off the good from the bad in what the convictions produced. They were indeed, as they claimed, involved with history. Consequently, the worst of their poems may only be read for the light they throw on their decade; but the study of their decade will continue to throw some light on even the best of their poems.

the Review Nos. 11/12

D

MARTIN DODSWORTH

BERNARD SPENCER

Bernard Spencer was fifty-three when he died in an accident in 1963; his second book of poems, *With Luck Lasting*, had only just been published. It received little notice, and despite the efforts of the Third Programme and *The London Magazine* it is quite possible, things being what they are, that it will soon be forgotten. That would be a pity because Spencer was a good poet. He belongs, perhaps, with those writers who have cultivated a single talent rather than a handful—poets like Norman Cameron or Andrew Young—but that is not a place without honour. Spencer fills it with an authority that I find lacking in either Cameron or Young. Furthermore, his poetry is more clearly related to the poetry of his own generation than is the case with either of these other two; it achieves in its own clear way something that most of his contemporaries were fumbling for in their poems.

His first book did not appear until 1946, at so late an hour that you might think he didn't have much to do with the Thirties at all, especially as its title, *Aegean Islands*, smacks more of Mediterranean luxury than of social concern. But then we have some odd ideas about these poets anyway: for example, we relegate Dylan Thomas and George Barker to the Forties, as though they weren't as much part of the post-Eliot scene as Auden or MacNeice. No: Spencer was a poet of that generation all right—born the same year as Louis MacNeice, and first published noticeably in *New Verse*, of which he was for a while co-editor. The pedigree is impeccable.

Kenneth Allott has said that Spencer's poem "Allotments: April" "might very well represent the kind of poem for which *New Verse* stood: straightforward but unpedestrian language, feeling expressed through observation, intelligence reflecting on observation and awake to the implications of feeling." The poem is in part an attempt to revise literary convention; it is about spring, but spring is no longer "the only pretty ring-time", for now "love detonates like sap / Up into the limbs of men and bears all the seasons / And the starving and the cutting . . ."

We have given up songs of spring, and our sense of it is diminished further by our no longer believing in a God: "Lost to some of us the festival joy / At the bursting of the tomb . . ." April only means now the boys playing out of doors again and the gardeners working in the allotments:

> they make a pause in
> The wireless voice repeating pacts, persecutions,
> And imprisonments and deaths and heaped violent deaths,
> Impersonal now as figures in the city news.

It cannot expunge the poet's consciousness of "real poverty, / The sour doorways of the poor";

> Rather it adds
> What more I am; excites the deep glands
> And warms my animal bones as I go walking
> Past the allotments and the singing water-meadows. . . .

It is not only the qualities of observation and intelligence noted by Mr. Allott, or the way the poem works against literary convention, or its awareness of "real poverty", that makes it typical of its time (it was printed in *New Verse* for June–July 1936); it is also the very structure and conclusion of the poem "Rather it adds . . ."

"Allotments: April" begins with a question: "In what sense am I joining in / Such a hallooing, rousing April day . . .?" After the question, possible answers are rejected, for the old ways of thinking about the season are outdated. The poet's situation is described, and finally an answer is given. Spring is no longer seen as a force that transforms sensation; it merely adds to existing sensations the sense of "what more I am". Just as the feeling of spring is reduced by the poet to the same level as other feelings, so the poem's conclusion seems to have an equal weight with its other parts. It is equally important for the poet to say what April is not as what it is. There is an equal stress on the descriptive part of the poem as there is on the part which attempts to answer the question which ostensibly prompts the poem. Finally, there is an impression of arbitrariness in the order of the parts of the poem that separate the question from its answer, and this may be attributed to the poet's refusal to value one rejected answer above another. He wants his rejected answers, as it were, side by side. I would like to argue that this poetry of addition, as it might be termed, derives from the general

tendency of the Thirties poets to employ catalogues of objects or similes
in their poems, and especially from the kind of feeling that drove them
to do this.

   These poets were attempting to make the subject of their poetry a
vastly more complicated world than had for a century or so seemed to
be in its affinities poetic. They wanted to get into their poems direct
experience of a largely mechanised society viewed in the light of current
political and psychological theory, and that implied, in effect, a development of poetic practice in two directions at once. Firstly they had to
extend the subject-matter of their poems to include a way of life under
industrial conditions to a large extent unfamiliar to their likely readers,
if not to themselves; and secondly they had to develop a style capable
of expressing the complication and depth of motive which had brought
that way of life into being. Day Lewis's *Magnetic Mountain* is a good
example of the poet's staking of claims in new territory; so is Charles
Madge's poem "Drinking in Boulton", with its curious air of being a
report from country hitherto unexplored:

> Not from imagination I am drawing
> This landscape (Lancs), this plate of tripe and onions. . . .

A lot of the poetry was a kind of literary equivalent to Mass Observation: a poetry that accumulated detail in the present tense, adding clause
to clause in a theoretically endless because arbitrarily related series:

> The streets are brightly lit; our city is kept clean:
> The third class have the greasiest cards, the first play high;
> The beggars sleeping in the bows have never seen
> What can be done in staterooms; no one asks why.
>   (W. H. Auden, "The Ship")

If one wanted to group the poets of the 'thirties in a way that would
make useful generalisations possible, it would not be utterly foolish to
distinguish between those who, like Empson or Dylan Thomas, employed a syntax that was complex, argumentative and intensive, and
those who, like Auden or MacNeice, used syntax that was simple and
direct, but sought to hint at the intricacy of their subject matter by
leaving the relation of statements to each other obscure. Auden, it is
true, is a poet of such large sympathies that it is hard to pin him down
to one method rather than another. Nevertheless, the cumulative style

has played an important part in the development of his verse. It is, after all, the foundation of "Spain":

> Yesterday all the past. The language of size
> Spreading to China along the trade-routes: the diffusion
>   Of the counting-frame and the cromlech;
> Yesterday the shadow reckoning in the sunny climates.
>
> Yesterday the assessment of insurance by cards,
> The divination of water, yesterday the invention
>   Of cart-wheels and clocks. . . .

Many of his recent poems, too, are indebted to this style of thinking and writing, since they consist largely of heaps of facts—the "Bucolics" in *The Shield of Achilles*, for example, or more startlingly "Encomium Balnei" and "The Cave of Nakedness" (*Encounter*, August 1962 and December 1963).

Of course, to observe that the Thirties poets have such a rhetorical characteristic is to say nothing of the value of it poetically; the *kind* of use to which it is put differs vastly with each poet. Generally, it seems that wherever speech was reduced to a series of names of objects or simple statements not obviously connected by discursive logic it became necessary for the poet to emphasise the tone of voice in which he was speaking; both the examples from Auden show this. There is a similar stress laid in those poems of MacNeice that demonstrate this cumulative style; "Bagpipe Music" is almost entirely a matter of the tone of voice:

> It's no go the picture palace, it's no go the stadium,
> It's no go the country cot with a pot of pink geraniums,
> It's no go the Government grants, it's no go the elections,
> Sit on your arse for fifty years and hang your hat on a pension.

There is no argument or progression here; the poem depends for its success entirely on the voice that we catch between the lines. The poem stands still as the music gets wilder and wilder—that is the point. But it needn't be; other poems pile up names and statements without this frenetic effect, and almost disguise the fact that the same device is being used:

> Down in Europe Seville fell,
> Nations germinating hell,

> The Olympic games were run—
> Spots upon the Aryan sun.
> And the don in me set forth
> How the landscape of the North
> Had educed the saga style
> Plodding forward mile by mile.
>
> ("Postscript to Iceland")

The point about the way cumulative effects are used by the Thirties poets is that they resist being pinned down as part of one mode of expression at all because they can be made to serve so many different ends. For example, it would be tempting to explain their use as springing from the comparatively simple attitudes politically committed poets had to express; continually to add to the non-essential, non-argumentative parts of a poem might be a means of hiding the crudity of emotion and paucity of ideas implicit in the committed message. This might be true of "Spain", for example, though one can applaud both the superficial liveliness of the poem and its right-mindedness; it might be even truer of Spender's "Vienna". But one has to bear in mind other uses of the trick: for instance, the effect is not simple in the conclusion of a poem like Michael Roberts's "Elegy for the Fallen Climbers":

> The pause, the poise between two worlds, returning—
> Rivers, communications, railroads, frontiers,
> The valley, and white saxifrage and gentians,
> Soft evening light upon the lower hills,
> Returning—
>
> The chouca turning in the air, the dazzling ice,
> The massive broken peak, the world unfolded.
> Darkness like an anguish, falling,
> The eyes, the fingers black with frostbite,
> The substance or the shadow, turning, twisting?

The landscape is at least half Auden—valley, frontier and gentians—but the intonation is Roberts's; far more even than the grating repetitions of "Bagpipe Music" these lines depend on our noticing the kind of voice that underlies their grammatical haziness. The gradual mounting-up to an indefinite conclusion—"turning, twisting?"—is parallel to the oncome of "Darkness like an anguish falling", but the parallel is not made explicit in this series of phrases like beads on a string. Faced by a descriptive technique used for such different purposes as we find in Roberts and MacNeice, we must be content with the explanation that it derives from the poets' awareness of a wider world to look at, in the largest sense; a similar explanation can be offered for the similar technique in Whitman. It is not a striking generalisation, but it does not risk too much.

"Allotments: April" uses the cumulative style in a way that suggests on the part of the poet the discovery of a hitherto uncomprehended complexity in his feelings, together with an apparently artless honesty that withholds nothing from the reader. "Rather it adds / What more I am . . ." Spring is Spencer's consciousness of his own self set off against his awareness of things that call him out of himself—"imprisonments and deaths" and "real poverty"—and he sees it as part of a larger movement in the world of which he is only one inhabitant. The personal conclusion and tone of voice suggest the individual, whilst the collection of descriptive facts suggests the world in which the individual is only another fact. The poem depends on the balance of these para-doxical feelings, and employs an equalising style to express them; finally, it evades any false solution to the paradox by a beautiful, gliding movement that passes from the individual to the nature that surrounds him to the nature that echoes his situation ambiguously:

> April warms my animal bones as I go walking
> Past the allotments and the singing water-meadows
> Where hooves of cattle have plodded and cratered, and
> Watch today go up like a single breath
> Holding in its applause at masts of height
> Two elms and their balanced attitude like dancers,
>   their arms like dancers.

"Once in Greece he started to carve out quite new kinds of poem, and indeed it is within the context of Greece that his work is best judged." Spencer went to Greece in 1938, and it is true that from that date on his poems are immediately recognisable as his; yet we don't need to concur with the second half of what his friend Lawrence Durrell has to say. His development owes as much to the English literary scene in spirit as it does to the Greek and Mediterranean landscape in subject-matter. The intensity of the Southern light and atmosphere seems to have driven

him to an extreme objectivity in his verse that almost squeezes personality out of the poem. But there is always the poet's special tone of
voice to assure us that his interest is a human one.

"Aegean Islands 1940–41" is a fine example of his mature style:

> Where white stares, smokes or breaks,
> Thread white, white of plaster and of foam,
> Where sea like a wall falls;
> Ribbed, lionish coast,
> The stony islands which blow into my mind
> More often than I imagine my grassy home. . . .

Initially the reader is faced with the external scene, but one in which the
light is so dazzling that only white is to be made out as it "stares,
smokes or breaks". The next line resolves this whiteness into the plaster
of walls, the foam on the sea, and the thread of cloth; the dominant
visual effect is maintained by the conjunction of "white, white", and
the rhythm, which is strongly stressed but irregular, suggests the way
in which the white objects named compete for our attention in the
general impression. They even compete for the functions named in the
preceding line—the thread and plaster could either stare or break, the
foam smokes and breaks also. They compete, but there is no winner;
without diminishing our sense of the actuality of any of them, Spencer
suggests an equal balance between them. The cumulative style is used
to create ambiguous relations between the units perceived, and by this
to suggest an unlaboured, unthinking unity in both perception and
style of living. The "sea like a wall falls" because foam and plaster are
akin in their whiteness, as are the sea ("The weaving sea" Spencer calls
it later in the poem) and the thread of the sails on its surface.

The very syntax of the poem suggests suspension; the main clause
only begins after eighteen lines of infinitives and descriptive clauses:

> All these were elements in a happiness
> More distant now than any date like '40
> A.D. or B.C. ever can express.

The suspension is not only the balance between elements in that life—

> To know the gear and skill of sailing,
> The drenching race for home, and the sail-white houses

—but also the discontinuity and sense of "distance" between then and
now, between the poet's voice and the actuality of what is only

remembered: a discontinuity implicit in the cumulative style and used in a quite different way in "Allotments: April". The parenthesis "A.D. or B.C." in the last line, unexpected because a superfluous addition to what is being said if regarded logically, suggests a final "suspension"— the paradox of a way of life that has barely altered despite two thousand years of human history. History seems only a parenthesis, or the interval between the poet and the eternal present (the *infinitives* and the present tense descriptive clauses) of his Aegean islands. The war which separates him from them is ephemeral compared with "The stony islands which blow into my mind".

Writing about Auden in 1937, Spencer praised him for "brutalising his thought and language to the level from which important poetry proceeds". His own verse also attempts this brutality; he believed that "more sophisticated poetry, if it is to have any force, has also to be rooted in the uncivilised layers of the mind, where what is ugly and what is beautiful can both be contemplated and do not exclude each other." The distancing effect of "Aegean Islands 1940–41" has to do with this being rooted where "what is ugly and what is beautiful can both be contemplated". Here we encounter yet another paradox. Although there is a distance between the poet and what he describes at a superficial level, there is deeper down a sense of identity—the enduring life of "the stony islands which blow into my mind" is identified with the part of him that can reject the war as ephemeral.

In Spencer's poetry the superficial display of personality and emotion is avoided, whilst an overall tone of voice reminds us that anything said bears a direct relation to the observing and quietly organising mind. The accumulation of descriptive detail appears to be an impersonal, unjudging process, whilst the elements of what is accumulated can in fact be subject to most stringent control by the poet. Spencer avoided the poetry of obvious attitudes and emotion. "Pity and disgust and the scientific attitude are all attitudes of separation, not of joining." By underplaying the self-consciousness of emotion which separates man from the rest of the created universe, he sought to reawaken an awareness of that universe and man simply at his ease in it. "True poetry is a dance in which you take part and enjoy yourself." His poetry was brutal because it purported to present the reader with a vision of the world unrefined by intelligence, and like most Rousseauistic writing the

D*

intellectual substructure of his work is large. The cumulative descriptions of his verse derive from Auden, but the kind of impersonality it
implies comes from Eliot and the symbolists, and the "brutality" idea
goes even further back.

August parentage guarantees nothing. Spencer's bad poems fail often
because they are incoherent sketches that come to no conclusion or
point of balance. But his good poems centre on an important topic and
treat it with some subtlety. An unremarkable poem from the recent
collection that makes this theme clear is "Fluted Armour":

> Bored and humbled by every disintegrating day,
> because, meaningless, the wine-glass and the storm-cloud stayed
> particular things:
> having, as everyone must, lost my way;
> I went to the National Gallery to trade
> a confusion of particulars
> for what you might call a philosophy, for
> the world-gaze of the great Italians, and was not
> disappointed returning by Charing Cross Road, dazed
> by particular things:
> the narrowed eyes and caught breath of the archers in
>   Pollaiuolo's "San Sebastian",
> the smiling lips of Bronzino's "Venus",
> and in Piero di Cosimo's "Florentine General"
> the cold smite of the fluted armour my finger-tips had grazed.

The work of art restores our sense of the beauty and coherence of
"particular things"; the poem moves from a "confusion of particulars"
to "what you might call a philosophy". That last phrase doesn't strike
the ear kindly, a cliché from the Englishman's stock of ready-made
attitudes; occasional lapses of the kind are the almost inevitable
consequence of the unstudied air Spencer wished to give his style. The
vers libre is a rhythmical counterpart to the easiness of being the poem is
meant to convey; and the odd, occasional rhyming—"dazed" /
"grazed" is especially striking—is an ingenious equivalent for the
fortuitous beauties and rhymes of nature.

The slight air of chilly aestheticism about this poem is unusual;
especially in the later poems the personal tone is clear and humane—
"Delicate Grasses", for example, is about resisting the attraction

exercised by the non-life of things and the sense of liberation they give the poet:

> There is no name for such strong liberation;
> I drift their way; I need what their world lends;
> then, chilled by one thought further still than those,
> I swerve towards life and friends
> before the trap-fangs close.

The simplicity and economy of statement leave no room for doubt about the truth of the statement; there is no rhetoric, except the last line, which looks back on the whole poem, as it were. As in "Aegean Islands 1940–41", there is no main verb until the last stanza is reached; an unpopulated scene is described detail by detail, almost hypnotically, and the last stroke is to change our view altogether. The last line causes us to swerve also, to reconsider

> Cool water jetting from a drinking fountain
> in crag-lands, miles from peopled spot,
> year upon year with its indifferent flow;
> sound that is and is not;
> the wet stone trodden low.

To multiply examples of Spencer's work is only too easy, but it should be enough to suggest why it is one might want to read him. The acute sense in him of an underlying unity and an all too obvious division, between lovers, between man and the world in which he lives, between what seems and what is, gives his poetry a greater humanity than the work of more self-consciously descriptive poets like Charles Tomlinson or William Carlos Williams. He applies to emotion the same eye that perceives the world of sea and islands, and he sees correspondences between the natural and the human world that are consoling because they are seen by an observer so truthful. In "Sud-Express" the description of the world flying past a train-window becomes a description of the levels at which life is lived:

> We pelt the way we came with houses, saplings, flowers;
> the middle fields swing, boil back and stream like lava;
> forests of distance shake their necks and gallop with us.

It is his refusal to simplify that makes this triple vision possible for him; it is his willingness to add one thing to another, until the profusion of objects has something of the enhancing confusion of the natural world itself. The first clue to this way of writing came from the poems of his contemporaries; the second, perhaps, from Seferis, some of whose poems were translated from the Greek by Spencer, Lawrence Durrell and Nanos Valaoritis and published in 1948 as *The King of Asine*. One of the poems there very well sums up Spencer's own aims: it is "Old Man on the River Bank":

> I want only to speak simply, to be given this grace,
> Because the song has been loaded with so much music that
>   little by little it is sinking.
> And we have decorated our art so much that its face has
>   been eaten away by the gold. . . .

The poetry of addition, the cumulative style, is the simplest descriptive style conceivable, and lends to Spencer's poems the force of a river or a dance:

> That great advancing meaning among the herbs and weeds,
> Among the grazing beasts which drink, men who sow and reap.
> Among great tombs and small habitations of the dead—
> That current which goes its way, not so different from the
>   blood of men. . . .

Reading his poems reminds one that the Thirties was not a time of entirely political verse but of some of the most humanely concerned poetry in English.

the Review Nos. 11/12

COLIN FALCK

PHILIP LARKIN

The hero of Philip Larkin's first novel dreams up a girl called Jill, and then tries to identify this beautiful unreality with a real girl who in some ways resembles her. The result is comic and sometimes very moving, but in terms of making contact with the real girl it is not a success.

Real life seems never to have borne very much relation to the idea that Larkin wanted to have of it, and the progress of his poetry since *The North Ship* is a kind of steady exorcising of romantic illusions, an ever-deepening acceptance of the ordinariness of things as they are. Or if not as they are, at least as they might seem to be, beyond all their dashed hopes and "unreal wishes", to ordinary people. And yet at the same time the unreal wishes have continued to haunt this ordinary world and to make everything in it seem stale and impoverished.

Larkin's poems have nearly always turned on ideas, above all on ideas of love and death, and one of the differences between *The Whitsun Weddings*★ and the earlier books is that the ideas themselves are now presented without very much poetic adornment. Death, which was once

> a black-
> Sailed unfamiliar, towing at her back
> A huge and birdless silence

can now appear simply as "the only end of age" or "what is left to come"; and "that much-mentioned brilliance, love" is in fact mentioned by name a great many times throughout *The Whitsun Weddings*. The effect of this is to give real strength to some of the more autobiographical poems, and in "Dockery and Son", perhaps the best of these, the reflection on death grows out of the opening personal situation with a terrible bareness and clarity:

> Where do these
> Innate assumptions come from? . . .
> . . . looked back on, they rear

★ *The Whitsun Weddings*. Philip Larkin. Faber & Faber, 1964.

> Like sand-clouds, thick and close, embodying
> For Dockery a son, for me nothing.
> Nothing with all a son's harsh patronage.
> Life is first boredom, then fear.
> Whether or not we use it, it goes,
> And leaves what something hidden from us chose,
> And age, and then the only end of age.

The starkness of these lines (and the way the poem breaks metre to accommodate them) seems to me something quite new in Larkin's poetry.

But this courting of abstract ideas has another result which is not so encouraging. It intensifies, almost to the point of absoluteness, the contrast between life as it is and life as it might (impossibly) be if only everything were different. And I think this may be the real difference between *The Whitsun Weddings* and the earlier poetry. It is love, more than anything else, which seems to concentrate our dreams of another and better life:

> In everyone there sleeps
> A sense of life lived according to love.
> To some it means the difference they could make
> By loving others, but across most it sweeps
> As all they might have done had they been loved.

Love promises "to solve, and satisfy, / And set unchangeably in order", and it should fall on us, "they say", "Like an enormous yes". Even the Modes for Night section of the large cool store can remind us "How separate and unearthly love is". Love, in fact, has to bear the heaviest load of our unreal wishes. But the contrast between the ideal and the ordinary is to be seen elsewhere too, and the "sharply-pictured groves / Of how life should be" in the poem about advertising have echoes in many other places. The girl in the "Sunny Prestatyn" poster was "too good for this life". Home is "A joyous shot at how things ought to be, / Long fallen wide". And all through the book there is a sense of "our live imperfect eyes / That stare beyond this world".

The title of the advertising poem, "Essential Beauty", is really more than a joke, because what all this adds up to is a kind of Platonism. Goodness, truth and beauty are not really to be found in the human world at all. The counterpart of such impossible idealism is that real human existence comes to seem quite meaningless. Even brute nature has its own laws and order, and even "our flesh / Surrounds us with its own decisions": but we can never share in this order ourselves. We remain

> ignorant of the way things work:
> Their skill at finding what they need,
> Their sense of shape, and punctual spread of seed,
> And willingness to change.

Our own lives are simply a "unique random blend / Of families and fashions". If we dedicate ourselves to finding out the meaning of things we shall end up watching

> the hail
> Of occurrence clobber life out
> To a shape no one sees

and with our faces "bent in / By the blows of what happened to happen". When we finally learn the mistake of having

> spent youth
> Tracing the trite, untransferable
> Truss-advertisement, truth

and discover that books are a load of crap, etc., half life is over and it is too late even to enjoy ourselves.

It is easy enough to sympathise with all this: perhaps everything really is pretty hopeless. But futile though life may be for the majority of people in our present society, it is not futile in principle in the way that Larkin makes it seem. By coming to rest so easily in this necessity, the necessity of life's meaninglessness, Larkin's poetry is most of the time a poetry of consolation. The grip of this deadening philosophy is not yet complete, though, and there are many poems where it is qualified or even held off altogether. It is this that makes "The Whitsun Weddings" itself so unusual. The end of this poem, with its thought "of London spread out in the sun, / Its postal districts packed like squares of wheat", its sense of "the power / That being changed can give", and its final image of the "arrow-shower / Sent out of sight, somewhere becoming rain", it unlike anything else in the book and succeeds, however fragilely, in overcoming the usual despair. Another poem, "Reference Back", concludes with the reflection that

> Truly, though our element is time,
> We are not suited to the long perspectives
> Open at each instant of our lives.
> They link us to our losses: worse,
> They show us what we have as it once was,
> Blindingly undiminished, just as though
> By acting differently we could have kept it so.

There is disillusion enough here, and yet there is hope too: the long perspectives are at least open, and the two very personal stanzas which lead up to this sad conclusion make it more of a reflection on one particular life than a judgement on life in general.

It is the autobiographical poems which stand up to Larkin's philosophy best, in fact. By developing out of a personal situation it can take on an existential force for the poet himself without at the same time imposing itself on everyone. This comes out best of all, perhaps, in "Dockery and Son", where the poem as a whole is so personal that the summing-up line "Life is first boredom, then fear" has all the force of a personal cry. In a poem like "Love Songs in Age", on the other hand, the poet is writing about someone else, and for all his sensitivity to this person's feelings at a particular moment the result is somehow generalised and sentimental: the sense of loss remains pure nostalgia, leading nowhere, and we may even find ourselves resenting the poet's too-easy familiarity with it in another person. When the emptiness and futility of the other person's life is as complete as it is in "Mr. Bleaney", of course, this question hardly arises: the sadness of Bleaney is that his life really can be summed up in his landlady's remarks and the few bits and pieces of his "one hired box", and the only feelings we really experience are the poet's own incomprehension of what it must have felt like to be Bleaney and his horror at how much he has in common with him. The poem where Larkin comes nearest to capturing someone else's experience without being either patronising or sentimental is probably "Afternoons". The description here is precise and delicate—not least through being in free verse instead of the usual iambics—and goes well beyond a mere notation of the scenery:

> Summer is fading:
> The leaves fall in ones and twos
> From trees bordering
> The new recreation ground

In the hollows of afternoons
Young mothers assemble
At swing and sandpit
Setting free their children.

The degree of identification seems exactly right in this poem, and even in the concluding lines the language is poetic, interpreting the young mothers' situation without imposing any judgement on it:

Their beauty has thickened.
Something is pushing them
To the side of their own lives.

There is something of Rilke's *Neue Gedichte* in this poem: it shows the rather special kind of success which is possible when the poet sets himself to write about the emotions of people he does not know. But it also shows how delicately this has to be done.

It is interesting that none of the poems in *The Whitsun Weddings* is autobiographical in the fullest sense—in the sense, that is, of presenting the poet as a poet and not simply as his usual bachelor persona. This is not surprising perhaps, because there is really no room for poets in the Platonic world that Larkin has committed himself to. In most of the poems which describe the world of ordinary people the poet appears either as an observer or not at all. In the one poem which is explicitly about the poet *qua* poet ("Send No Money") the concrete world itself disappears, and the result is a kind of moral tale, more than a little vicious in tone. (Compare this with its equivalent in *The Less Deceived*, "Reasons for Attendance".) The effectiveness of a poem like "Dockery and Son" comes in part from our awareness that the real man present is also a poet; but there is no indication of this in the poem (beyond the fact that it was written at all) and we really have to supply the information for ourselves.

I think Larkin's general conception of truth and reality accounts for much that is typical in his style. In all the poems in *The Whitsun Weddings* there is an extreme propriety of syntax and language which seems to have intellectual clarity as its ideal and to regard metaphor as something rather special. When the poems do leave the level of basic description it is most often by means of explicit simile. The effect of this is to preserve the appearance of language as somehow in itself literal and to lodge the poetry self-consciously in a grammatical device:

> Its postal districts packed like squares of wheat
>
> Here silence stands like heat
>
> As if out on the end of an event

But the distinction here is very rough, of course (and there would not be much room for poetry if it were otherwise). Who can say whether "Summer is fading" is literal or metaphorical? The point is only that Larkin writes most of the time as though the distinction was quite clear. And yet his most impressive lines actually come when he allows himself to unbend and to submit to more or less pure metaphor:

> Dark towns heap up on the horizon

Some of the most beautiful lines of all are in fact very meticulous in their grammar:

> A sense of falling, like an arrow-shower
> Sent out of sight, somewhere becoming rain.
>
> An immense, slackening ache,
> As when, thawing, the rigid landscape weeps

But their real power is in the metaphor they carry: "an arrow-shower ... somewhere becoming rain", "the rigid landscape weeps".

These last examples are revealing in another way too. For want of any overall texture of metaphor, Larkin's poems usually fall into a pattern of description-plus-evaluation: it is nearly always the sum-marising argument which holds the poem together. (His earlier tech-nique, on the other hand, was very often to build from a single meta-phor, carrying it right through the poem like an argument.) One result of this is that it becomes necessary to attempt direct descriptions of emotions themselves, almost as if these were simply another kind of object, to be observed and recorded along with all the objects of the external world. The last two examples are both descriptions of this kind: of "a sense of falling", of "an immense slackening ache". That Larkin pushes through to poetry here is not surprising, perhaps, because it is only at points like these that this general approach permits of any subjectivity at all. If emotions are to be described, then it is crucial that they should be described well. But would it not be better to give up the general approach itself? It is not really a poem's job to describe emotions, any more than it is its job (merely) to describe anything else. A poem is an *expression* of an emotion, but this is quite another thing: it does not demand that any emotions should be mentioned at all. A poem can express emotion without talking about anything but trees or cities or other people. The very way in which Larkin succeeds in his direct attempts to describe emotions actually demonstrates the case against his method as a whole: in both of the above examples an emotion is finally expressed through a metaphor which takes in the outside world—"the rigid landscape weeps", "an arrow-shower ... somewhere becoming rain"—and which carries a subjectivity deeper than any "sense of falling" or "immense slackening ache". There are times, on the other hand, when Larkin's most descriptive-looking lines do quiver towards a real intensive meaning. When he describes the women in "Faith Healing"—

> Moustached in flowered frocks they shake

—there is a genuine subjectivity in the description, and its effect is to make the accompanying reflection and philosophising seem almost unnecessary.

This basically descriptive approach, depending as it does on argument rather than the individual moment of perception, makes it easy to understand Larkin's adherence to very regular metres and rhyme-schemes. But it also goes some way to explaining that other hallmark of his style, the doubled adjective. "Frank submissive", "immense slackening", "unique random", "sweet commissioned": at their best they are words which have a good deal of tension between their central meanings, and they get their effect by being juxtaposed within a grammatical form which would as a rule be simply descriptive ("big red", etc.) or else banal ("wise old", etc.). It is one of the few imaginative techniques that remain for the poet who has committed himself to an external-descriptive view of language and the avoidance of metaphor.

I have said that Larkin's poetry is for the most part a poetry of consolation. In an article on "Poetry and Landscape in Present England" (*Granta*, 19 Oct. 1963) Donald Davie has praised Philip Larkin for the "humanism" with which he identifies himself with the ordinary life of this most industrialised of societies. "Precisely", Davie says, "because poem after poem since *The Waste Land* has measured our present (usually seen as depleted) against our past (usually seen as rich) Larkin's refusal to do this is thoroughly refreshing—at last, we recognise with relief, we can take all that for granted, take it as read." It seems to me that this is a mistake. There is not much doubt, perhaps, that the landscape of present-day England is more completely dominated by the urban-industrial way of life than that of any other country. But to extol the kind of poetry which takes this as its starting point and retains no serious urge to make discriminations is to surrender in advance to the scientific nightmare. By all means let us not retreat into the "nature" world of plants and animals and forget about humanity. But unless we are able to find and choose the natural from the unnatural in human life itself we are surely lost. We can accept modern civilisation in its entirety, as Larkin seems to, or we can reject it equally entirely (as the school of Leavis comes near to doing); but either way we are refusing the real choice between life and death, between good and evil. And if we do this, what we have to say will no longer seem very relevant to the people who still make these choices in their lives, because what we are refusing is human existence as such. Larkin has probably captured the feel of life as it is for a great many ordinary people much of the time, and this gives his poetry a certain kind of humanity. But he has done this only at the expense of a deeper and more important humanity, because he has done it ultimately at the expense of poetry. No doubt it is always important to maintain some general sense of what most other people's lives are like. But the poet cannot be content with this, and it might even be argued that it is not really his business *qua* poet at all, whatever might be expected of him as a novelist or as a human being. If there is really no beauty or truth or love to be found in the concrete here-and-now, however it might appear to ordinary people, then there is surely none to be found anywhere. The "other" Platonic truth, if it exists at all, is only the order which is to be found in the real world of existing things, and it is the poet, above all, who can be expected to find this order; and he will find it in his own experience. So that by identifying himself with the drab, fantasy-haunted world of the waste land Larkin has not only downgraded the whole of real existence against an impossible absolute standard, but has also cut the ground from under the poet's feet. The fantasy-world which he has elected to share has little to do with romanticism, because it destroys the very bridge which romanticism would construct between the ideal and the world which actually exists: the poet can no longer do anything to bring our dreams into relation with reality. The ideal, for Larkin, has become inaccessible, and being inaccessible it can only throw the real world into shadow instead of lighting it up from within. In the typical landscape of Larkin's poems the whole chiaroscuro of meaning, all polarities of life and death, good and evil, are levelled away. Farms, canals, building-plots and dismantled cars jostle one another indiscriminately—the view from the train window, with its complete randomness and detachment, is at the heart of Larkin's vision—and all of them are bathed in the same general wistfulness. There are no epiphanies. Love and death, though they are the controlling ideas of the poems, can never inflame the individual moments of existence; instead they simply diminish them, and the boredom of this diminished existence is invested with a kind of absolute necessity.

That Larkin himself is not oblivious to these questions is clear enough; and indeed no one really could be. The short poem "Water" ("If I were called in / To construct a religion / I should make use of water . . .") shows that he is able to see things symbolically and not only as part of the modern landscape; but there is a coyness about this poem which makes it hard to take very seriously. Asked to prophesy, I should see two possible lines of development in *The Whitsun Weddings*. The first is in the autobiographical bareness of "Dockery and Son", the second in the delicacy of a poem like "Afternoons". That the first can lead somewhere is clear enough from, for example, Robert Lowell's *Life Studies*; but I think it points ultimately to a dead end. This kind of bare utterance ("Life is first boredom, then fear", "My mind's not right", "I have wasted my life", etc.) must somehow, if it is to remain poetry and not psychology, maintain some outlet to the real world and be set off by an external vision of things. It is this which the second alternative promises more directly, both in its quality of language and in its relatively free verse form. Larkin has found a new kind of directness in this book, and some of his earlier single-metaphor poems now look decorative and "poetic" by comparison. But when the metaphor itself was open enough ("No Road" is one of the best) they could carry a richness of vision which it would be a pity to lose altogether ("To watch that world come up like a cold sun ..."). I should like to think that something of this vision might now find its way into poems basically as simple and direct as "Afternoons".

In rejecting Larkin's particular brand of "humanism" I may seem to be asking for the kind of "right wing" violence to which D. H. Lawrence was sometimes led. I think perhaps I am. The last and truest humanism in art is the truthful expression of emotion, and this is something prior to all questions of politics: it concerns only the honesty or the corruption of our own consciousness. If this means barbarism, then let us have barbarism. Barbarism has come to be associated with obscurity, but no true expression can be really obscure. Let us have lucid barbarism. If we cannot face it in art, we shall have to face it soon enough in life. Should we really, in this post-Nazi age, be dismissing "solemn-sinister wreath-rubbish" in a piece of light verse? And does the Modes for Night counter really show "How separate and unearthly love is"?

the Review, No. 14

GABRIEL PEARSON

JOHN BERRYMAN

At a very primary level John Berryman's poetry worries me. Partly it's a matter of the way his energies are distributed and organised. There are passages which seem to suffer from a kind of verbal thrombosis: clots of syntax and metaphor and, consequently, areas drained, pallid and inert. One moment the gradient is angular and abrupt, the mental scramble demanded vertiginous. Next moment, we descend slopes of too smooth incline down which nothing is busy happening. I do not, however, want to translate this worry into a judgement. It is probably too visceral for that. I prefer to postpone questions of value until I have habituated myself to this poet's climate and world. This piece, then, will consist largely of the process of habituation.

Habituation, in my experience, consists of a kind of osmotic process by which the poems delicately seep into the reader's sensibility. Lines stick, whole poems establish a ghostly presence that demands frequent recourse for their greater realisation. I cannot say that this has really happened, even after several readings of the two Berryman volumes available in England. When lines have persisted—such as the much quoted "My love loves chocolate, she loves also me"—they have done so by too ostentatiously wearing the look of lines designed to vibrate, and it's that that I have remembered. On the other hand, the quality of mind, of sensibility, persists beyond what can be accounted for by current preoccupation. I am impressed by the thrust, if not always the organisation, of Berryman's energies. He is an ambitious, large-gestured poet, traditional in the importance he assigns the role of poet and idiosyncratic in his exercise of it. Idiosyncratic or genuinely original? That question is one part of the worry, and I haven't made up my mind which.

More ignobly, my worry is a fear of being taken for a ride. One wants so much to affirm, to admire, not to make mere negation out of judiciousness. Berryman is a poet whose poems seem already written in the light of their future explication. They are the product of an immensely erudite, literary self-consciousness. One wonders whether erudition couldn't reach to calculation: whether intensity, complexity, even qualities of compassion and insight couldn't be simulated, cooked up, synthesised in the horribly over-equipped lab of critical analysis. Is this a manufactured body of poetry, rather than the body or thrust of experience made articulate? Or, if this were the case, is it possible that this too is a mode of experience as genuine, in the final resort, as any other, and perhaps the only way for one kind of self-conscious man of our time to go?

One final worry over-rides all others. Berryman's poetics are at least a highly complicated piece of machinery, which hums, whirrs and rumbles without cease. Rarely, except in the last two poems of the first volume, does his verse reach into or create the audible silence which characterises the art which persists for us. Could it be that beneath the clatter there is not silence, but simply nothing, an immense banality or simple-mindedness that the clatter of the verbal machinery tries to drown out? Is complexity only, after all, complication? Does the whole show consist of amplified and distorted platitude? But most good literature is close to platitude. It evades it, recovers the banality for insight, by virtue of its power to re-occupy what habit, timidity and unconsciousness have vacated. It recovers it, moreover, in terms of the language and equipment of consciousness proper to its own age, and that makes for novelty. The question then is whether Berryman has redeemed and revitalised the banal or simply regarnished it for specially over-refined and jaded palates.

By way of a pilot-example take this stanza from "Homage to Mistress Bradstreet":

> Sacred & unutterable Mind
> flashing through the universe one thought,
> I do wait without peace.
> Eat my sore breath, Black Angel. Let me die.
> Body a-drain, when will you be dry
> And countenance my speed
> To Heaven's springs? lest stricter writhings have me declined.

This is Ann praying for death ("Black Angel") quickly to end her dropsical or haemorrhaging sickness. The first couplet is inert. "Flashing" seems rather tired. True, there is syntactical punning. The third line could take the first couplet as its object (if "wait" = "await") or be a separate statement. It is just this syntactical complication that arouses suspicions. It hardly does anything functionally. Is it perhaps there on the opportunistic principle that a sufficiently widely-spread net is bound to snare something? But it could be argued that this is not Berryman but his protagonist, that, syntax aside, this is the proper vocabulary of Ann's kind of religion. Actually, I doubt this. It reads more like a much later, vapid pantheism. One has to conclude that this is a case where the syntactical machinery compensates by clatter for the limpness of mere taken-up space.

The next four lines are a different matter. Ann's conceit on a dry dying that will refresh her with the waters of life seems to belong genuinely to her religious sensibility, the kind of thing she might have written had she achieved her proper poetry. The muscular recoil of the second part of the Alexandrine lashes vigorously like a virtual devil's tail. The compression of "Eat my sore breath" becomes a cry wrung out of a tortured complexity of feeling. I should add that this stanza represents Berryman at his sufficiently characteristic worst. My analsyis focuses, but does not resolve, my doubts. Clearly, Berryman can (but how consistently does he?) mask emptiness under activity. The same activity can also model and contour a highly energised complex of thought and emotion.

It cannot be, of course, a matter of passages, but of whole poems. Again I choose (because that is the poem which up till now has principally made Berryman's reputation) "Homage to Mistress Bradstreet". What that poem is about is, at least on the surface, sufficiently clear. The real question is what is it *for*? I have not been able to capitulate to it with the ease and fervour of some of its admirers ("the most distinguished long poem by an American since *The Waste Land*"—Edmund Wilson. Would Wilson have called anything "distinguished" thirty years ago? Alas, for the weariness of distinguished minds!) The unease lurks that this may be a mandarin version of the historical picturesque, more grimly empathetic, more fiercely accurate than, say, "The Ballad of the Revenge", "The Battle of Lepanto", or (nearer home) "The Courtship of Miles Standish". Like these, it offers costumed narrative. Like these it deals in the glamour of the glibly-familiarised remote. If

it is no more than this, then it is a meretricious exercise in nostalgia,
however wry, astringent, grainy.

I do in fact think it more than this, and it is in this "more" that I find
Berryman's originality. Its syntax, while it sometimes disguises weakness, is ultimately a form of control, making of the whole poem and of
Ann's life-span a gigantic sentence, a unit of meaning accessible to
imagination. Beyond this it has, in fact, extreme linguistic authenticity
of a kind impossible to a Tennyson or Longfellow, which carries it far
beyond nostalgia, beyond even empathy. Ann's authentic voice combines with the poet's controlling syntax to relate past to present in such
a way that the past becomes an origin (a "sourcing" is Berryman's
pregnant term) and the present a destiny. I shall attempt to make this
good later. For the present it is noteworthy that the originality of this
poem depends less on evoked qualities of experience than on an extreme
linguistic simulation. The poet turns medium and transmits with all the
historical awareness—and sheer knowledge—available a dead voice,
becomes—and the syntax is what organises its release—a mouthpiece.
In effect, the poet's voice and her husband's court and provoke the voice
of Ann in much the same way. Out of the multiplicity of voices a
substantial reality emerges, the fully embodied bathos become thereby
the pathos of the human situation.

Berryman is, I take it, a supremely linguistic poet. His mind is
thronged with a host of voices, of tunes, of styles, and the syntax is the
strenuous effort to compose them. He is, in the first place, a representative victim of the failure of that vital amnesia which, in the past, permitted through a blessed combination of arrogance and ignorance, new
or reformed or re-discovered styles to develop. The *musée imaginaire*
results in a simultaneous availability of all past styles. This easily leads
to a despair of ever, amid the din, discovering a unique utterance.
Originality often seems ingenuity in picking up the currently audible
voices. Some poets seem to have adopted the wrong voice or seem to
be in transit through a succession of voices in search of their own
(Robert Lowell?). Modern self-awareness is fearfully adept at mimicry,
even to the extent of producing variations on original themes which at
first sound original. I am not here canvassing the question of tradition.
Traditions work both by selection and exclusion. It supremely doesn't
make sense to be part of *all* traditions. The educated poet today labours

under the liability of being heir to all the ages and as a result disinherited of his own. The way out of this dilemma may well be a plunge into a strictly contemporary idiom or a calculated naiveté. Or it may reside in pushing through the dilemma to an extremity where it ceases to be a liability and becomes something both individual and generic.

Berryman has had the courage not to inhibit his linguistic self-consciousness but to develop it to the full. By adding voice to voice, simulation to simulation, he has succeeded in creating a viable body of experience. This experience is the assemblage of voices itself, a complex of attitudes, tones, tunes and styles which adds up, as it were, to the density of a life. Or, perhaps, is beginning to. Berryman's career still feels unachieved. One senses a quickening order only now beginning to be discovered. For this reason, I do not intend to treat *77 Dream Songs** as an achieved, self-sufficient work, but as part of a process which only makes satisfactory sense in terms of the forward stress of Berryman's development.

Berryman is represented in England by two volumes. The second is *77 Dream Songs*; the first is the volume titled, after the long poem of the same name, *Homage to Mistress Bradstreet*. Besides the long poem itself, the volume is divided into "Early Poems" and "Later Poems". Between them the two volumes seem to provide a pretty adequate conspectus of Berryman's work so far.

"Early Poems" strike me as a good example of ventriloquism rather than mediumship: in this case Berryman is the dummy. These poems, despite the assumed mannerisms, are thin and unresonant, dreary in their tonalities, and without adequate form to match the grand pretentiousness of their themes. Even the worst poems are not atrocious, but dull, hysterical lists, excitedly and dutifully rehearsing a litany of contemporary horrors in a sub-Auden mode. The fashionable 'thirties pre-occupations are all on show: history, mechanised politics, personal fantasy all dragging in harness a dirty, disillusioned and dangerous decade. But there are other poems which promise something more genuinely personal, not by self-assertion but by a kind of craftsmanly quiet care. The most successful of these is "The Animal Trainer", which exists in two versions, each of thirty-five lines, each diminishing from

* *77 Dream Songs*. John Berryman. Faber & Faber, 1964.

a stanza of eight lines (dropping a line every stanza) to a final stanza of one line; each version is identical in all but the last ten lines (and the punctuation of the twenty-fourth). Such a structure is elaborate, demonstrating early a characteristic Berryman tendency to a dualism of sentiment and vehicle, making good what orthodoxy denies, a form-content dichotomy, and so achieving, for the alert reader, a complication of voices. The poem is a dialogue between heart and head, body and soul, and art and life, so that the poem's form enacts its theme. The versions themselves are not opposing statements, but supplement each other, to produce a forward-leaning asymmetry. The last lines are: (1) ". . . You learn from the animals. You learn in the dark"; (2) ". . . Animals are your destruction and your will". "Will" becomes a kind of arrow-head quivering towards the future.

This poem is essentially programmatic. It announces a strategy ("learn in the dark") which "Early Poems" attempts but fails to execute. This strategy derives from a choice—of will against abstraction, the human situation against what may be religion or art. Society against History, the animal cry of humanity ("the animals are coupling, and they cry") in sex, hunger, fear, against civilised and traditional utterance, the basic against the superior. A familiar programme, and one to which Berryman can make only a theoretical response at this time. Despite himself, his human situation poems are over-fastidious, exercises in feeling done from the outside. Their very desperation is contrived. They fail because Berryman has found no voice in which to utter or transmit contemporary man. This failure is compounded by the fact that Berryman's own voice is not his own, but borrowed, assembled from the literary influences most audible in the decade. Few poets strike me as more glibly derivative in their early poems as Berryman. It is as though the 'thirties were writing a composite poetry and producing, not a splendid chaos, but the blandest of common denominators.

One has to infer the chronology of Berryman's poetry from the poems themselves. The concluding poem of "Early Poems" begins "On the night of the Belgium surrender . . ." (It could be retrospective.) The second poem of "Later Poems", "Canto Amor", recalls that "Three years already of the round world's war / Had rolled by stoned and disappointed eyes". (Tense, theme, makes this almost certainly retrospective.) This leaves a gap of perhaps three years. This gap—if my guess is right—signals a change in strategy.

"Early Poems" left Berryman with a poet's will and equipment, but without, for the poetry, a self and a world. "Later Poems", "Homage" and 77 *Dream Songs*, search for a way to create these. Through a multiplication, interrogation and assumption of many different voices, a self composes itself. Through mediumistic passivity before these voices a world begins to form. This is no longer old-fashioned romantic self-expression. It is neo-romantic self-creation. To some extent poets have always changed selves via poems as well as changed poems via selves. Berryman's way is the first, not the second, and perhaps the inevitable strategy of a poet who discovers himself disinherited of a fixed character or history and is too timid and honest to fabricate one. Berryman's poetic selfhood is a process, an accepted running game of pursuit, occupation and displacement. Its future is whatever the developmental tendencies of the poems themselves, in their creation, suggest.

The result is a variousness which may well lead to the judgement that Berryman is uneven. There are naturally disasters. Nothing in "Early Poems" is as incoherent and turgid as "Sonnet 25" or "Boston Common". Some poems attempt a premature final meditation on man's contemporary situation in the poet's own voice. These repeat the faults of "Early Poems" and sound theoretical and disembodied in their desperation ("The Enemies of the Angels"). The most successful poems are those in which the poet is a medium for someone else or addresses someone, even if only his Muse ("Canto Amor"). Yet no poem is a dramatic monologue. The selves are assumed by the poet, not projected for theatrical revelation of character. Berryman is not a dramatist, but a medium. Yet the voices that speak through him constitute his developing self. As these voices are incorporated (literally give the poet body, as Berryman gives body to the shade of Ann Bradstreet), Berryman's style, his poetic self, becomes more and more accommodating, muscular, flexible, inventive and idiosyncratic. As a style, it has no characteristic imagery, or tonality. Style exists as a compositional energy, a process of combustion and fusion, which synthesises the disconnected experiences, voices, visions of the modern world into a succession of structured events. Its main instrument is a simultaneously disruptive and reconstitutive syntax. This syntax extends beyond sentence structure to the whole poem, by way of stanzas (Berryman works almost entirely through stanzas) which are not the stabilising pulse of meditation, but rather stops, lacunae, anacoluthon, parentheses—part of the fierce modelling or invention of meaning. Berryman's loyalty to the stanza should not be put down to traditionalism. It is purely instrumental, a further means of fusing or composing voices.

To say that Berryman seeks to create a self and a world perhaps describes the process too abstractly. "Early Poems", for all their derivativeness, show him concerned to diagnose, in a traditional way, contemporary society in the light of American destiny. Simultaneously —though in that part of the volume these aims don't coincide—he seeks more than a self, something more like a representative life, that in its integrity and contingency will transcend the merely provisional rôle of poet. Society as destiny and self as completed life coincide beautifully in the figure of Ann Bradstreet. She partakes at the foundation of white America while the idea of its destiny is still simple and uncompromised ("Strangers & pilgrims fare we here / declaring we seek a City . . ."). Berryman's own pursuit of America narrows to a point where its baffling accretions, bifurcations and diversions have yet to begin. In this moment (also Ann's life-span) all subsequent America is incipient. Ann is not only in labour with her child but with the bewildering diversity of twentieth century industrial society as well. (I don't want to suggest that the two-stanza description of Ann's travail is allegorical. It is actual enough. But Ann's lifetime compresses many meanings. She is in travail with children, with children as symbol of or substitute for poems, with the "hard" but "green" American future, etc.)

I don't feel this to be a feeble-hearted relapse into primitivism. The poem has none of the vagueness of nostalgia. It is all actual, all literal. Berryman does not create the past to escape from the present. Rather he invokes it (as epic poets invoke the racial past in their descents into the underworld) as a measure of a partially completed destiny that has been lived. The integrity of Ann's life approximates to the grounds on which a more complex, contemporary integrity might be founded. It also provides the measure of today's disintegration, social and personal.

It is appropriate that Ann is also a poet. But her poetry failed to render her life and was indeed bizarrely inappropriate to it:

Versing, I shroud among the dynasties;
quaternion on quaternion, tireless I phrase
anything past, dead, far. . . .

Berryman is like most modern poets pre-occupied by the relationship of the career of art to life, how the one may falsify the other. Ann's poetry resides in her life. Her verses were a kind of false language. Berryman attempts, in a sense, to write Ann's proper poetry, to redeem her true, lost verse. Implicitly, this translates his own search for a genuine verse which will translate the true life of himself and his times and not "shroud among dynasties".

In composing "Homage", I suspect that Berryman, consciously or unconsciously, was seeking an epic form that would be American, densely particular and human ("I renounce not even ragged glances, small teeth, nothing . . .") and a prototype of the power of survival in a pattern of living that treats its own death as a destiny and can so prove a consolation and inspiration. The whole of the last stanza triumphantly celebrates the integrity of Ann's life ("O all your ages") and contrasts it with the poet's own more unstable existence ("lost candle"; "so long as I happen"). Ann's life is "still" (that great romantic pun)—a simultaneous motion-in-rest, that can be imaginatively grasped in the past but which eludes the present.

I read "Homage" then as a necessary stage in Berryman's career. He becomes the medium for another voice, and in the process breaks a barrier of solipsism that enables him to become sensitive to the voices of his own century, to make them his own. He has done this, however, not by recoiling from art to life, but by taking linguistic experience to its limits, making of it an instrument capable of transmitting as many voices as are available. It does not seek to become *the* American voice (as does Williams's), but all the voices, organised through the forward thrust of the poet's energies through his own life.

Berryman's search for the integral life leads him to probe humanity in its extremity—subjected to madness, torture, or death. Some of the best poems in "Later Poems" (all "The Nervous Songs", "The Long Home", "Scots Poem", "A Winter-piece to a Friend Away, Venice, 182—", to mention a few) are all *in extremis* poems. "Venice 182—", for example, exposes, through an Adolphe-like voice and setting, the death of romantic love, in both its historical and personal dimensions.

"The Long Home" tracks the dying minutes of a millionaire, Ivan Illyich, through his unlived lives back to his origin in a "Barefoot soul fringed with rime". (With the frost of dead experience, but garbed in the poet's re-creation of him in poetry, "rime".) "New Year's Eve", though not, I think, a good poem, makes the *in extremis* idea quite explicit. The old year dies in "tears & lust and a scale of lies". There is no common language to articulate the human condition ("Our loss of Latin fractured how far our fate"). Poets succumb to drink and narcissism, while society ("wealthy & casual as a holiday") encourages bad poetry ("Most of us are linsey- / woolsey workmen, grandiose, and slack". A very good description of "Early Poems", incidentally.) Self-knowledge is only the desperation of psycho-analysis ("the key to secrets") and the only social knowledge, "Kinsey". Hope lies in the power to articulate and in the self that articulation may discover:

> Undisguised
> We pray our tongues & fingers
> records records the strange word that blows suddenly and lingers.

The articulated self may well turn out to be the unselved and many-selved substance of our inauthenticity. If so, the poet should be it, be what he seems, be his disguises. I may be over-reading here in the light of *77 Dream Songs*, but this is what I get from

> Ages we have sighed,
> And cleave more sternly to a music of
> Even this sore word "genocide".
> Each to his own! Clockless & thankless dream
> And labour Makers, being what we seem.

"Clockless & thankless dream" is the business of creating poetry, but also a specifically modern poetry, a poetry *in extremis*, a poetry which is simultaneous fantasy and aspiration. New Year's Eve is a forward as well as backward facing occasion. It celebrates a survival, as well as a death. If there is a value in Berryman's work its name is survival. Selves, historical catastrophes, wives, exaltations, fame, religions, parents, dismemberments, illnesses and appetites are all survived, and their survival celebrated in *77 Dream Songs*. And so, in a sense, that volume is a kind of extended New Year's Eve party in which the new year is greeted, not for any specific ingredient of hope, but because it's there, waiting to be lived.

"The Nervous Songs" are clearly a trial run for *Dream Songs*, or maybe suggested them. Though apparently random in the voices they mediate, they do in fact exhaust most human rôles. These are: priest, artist (Gauguin), professor, primitive, man of action, martyr. Berryman's syntax squeezes each figure in turn until it emits its essence and resolves back into the poet. This sets the scene for a treatment of the human situation which will be at once more personal and yet more comprehensive. A parallel evolution of Berryman's art has developed to the point where he can be anyone or any number of ones simultaneously or successively without failure of nerve (is such failure implicit in the title "The Nervous Songs"?), though with plenty of fully exhibited strain, the strain being part of the question (how do we?) and the assertion (but we do!) survives our own and our society's disintegration.

77 Dream Songs has one major theme, as far as I can see: modern man in the modern world. Perhaps, though, its theme is itself, the defeat of sterility it represents, the lucky triumph of its getting written. The number 77 has clearly something talismanic about it which suggests both irrefrangibility and repeatability. But it does have unity of a kind and the faint hint of a structure. The first song is elegiac, bantering and tragic simultaneously. It suggests a lover's permanent quarrel with the universe:

> Huffy Henry hid the day,
> unappeasable Henry sulked. . . .
>
> Hard on the land wears the strong sea
> and empty grows every bed.

The sombre finality of the last couplet is to some extent qualified by the childlike vocabulary of the first—"huffy", "sulked". Henry is the grown man-child confronting his own mortality. His demands upon life are absurd ("unappeasable") and yet it is they that confirm his humanity. Right from the first words Berryman employs his characteristic double syntax. The first line reads: (1) Henry hid; (2) Henry concealed the day about him (and so, when he stopped, would manifest it again). The very first couplet is a kind of riddle. The riddle is really Berryman's "long / wonder that the world can bear and be" (can "endure"; can "procreate"). It is this "wonder" that the songs sing. Nothing is resolved. In the last song, "unappeasable" has turned into

E

"impenitent". Henry is prepared to go on living "in a world of Fall /
forever". The long wonder becomes wonder in a sense closer to
"miracle": "it is a wonder that . . . he's making ready to move on".
This could be signing a quietus. Henry is not the poet and Henry's
preparedness to die, if that is what the last line means, need not be the
poet's. But the line needn't imply a particular destination, but merely
the acceptance of process, the ability to shift without terminus. As
such, it is a thoroughly secular affirmation. It also marks a stage of
necessary disillusionment, which enables the poet to accept his role as a
poet on the condition that he will also be an interpreter, a mouthpiece,
a megaphone, aimed at a perhaps indifferent auditor:

> . . . p.a.'d poor thousands of persons on topics of grand
> moment to Henry, ah to those less & none.

He has reached the stage of Yeats's famous apology:

> Pardon that for a barren passion's sake,
> Although I have come close on forty-nine,
> I have no child, I have nothing but a book. . . .

but describes it more tersely:

> Wif a book of his in either hand
> he is stript down to move on.

The whole sequence describes the arc from the sombre withdrawal of
the first song to the guarded but emphatic affirmation of the last. The
same arc is implicit in many individual songs, by virtue of the inner
dialectic of jangling voices: Henry's, Henry as Bones, Negro, the poet's
own. For example, in the first song, Henry's sulks are deflated by the
poet's clinical and amused "I see his point—a trying to put things over".
(To get away with a false attitude, or to express his true feelings.) More
usually the duologue of Henry as straightman Bones and his unnamed
deflationary interlocutor (Negro) acts out the same triad (varied in
sequence) of withdrawal, deflation, affirmation. Henry as Bones I take
to be Henry in the full sense of his mortality. (The gravedigger started
digging the day Hamlet was born.) Song 26 ends, for example, with
the question and answer:

> —What happen, then, Mr. Bones?
> —I had a most marvellous piece of luck. I died.

This death occurs at the end of the first section of Songs (26) after Henry (or the poet) recounts yet again another version of Henry's life-history: innocence ("The glories of the world struck me, made me aria, once"— possibly "native wood-notes wild"; or I didn't need poetry because I *was* poetry), sexual experience and then, in recoil but suggesting a relationship between sex and art, poetry: "—Fell Henry back into the original crime: art, rime", which in turn involves fissured solipsism and a sense of society:

> besides a sense of others, my God, my God,
> and a jealousy for the honour (alive) of his country ...

Again the extreme hedged bet: is "my God, my God" a meaningless cry, a Job-like religious affirmation, or has God become secular devotion ("a sense of others")? This kind of use of dead oaths to suggest an emptiness that inherits only the forms of religion or betokens a search to renew those forms is a common device in dramatists like Beckett and Albee. In Beckett it seems to be the ache of absent theology. Albee, more secular, a reflex twitch of human paralysis. *77 Dream Songs* resembles Albee more than Beckett, but the dialectic of voices which is really one split voice trying to unify itself, is common to all three. Berryman uses "Dream" in *77 Dream Songs* in just the ambiguous way that Albee does in *The American Dream*. Dream equals unreality, fantasy (personal and national); dream equals aspiration, hope (personal and national). *77 Dream Songs* is actually more ebullient than either Albee or Beckett. The stage is habitually a supreme expression of human concourse; the poet's study, or tower, of isolation. Albee's stage swops with Berryman's study: the one depressedly isolated, the other uncharacteristically thronged.

After Henry's Death (Song 26) he lives on for another fifty-one songs. Berryman's point seems to be that physical death is only one of a whole series of deaths or perhaps, in the end, isn't a death at all if the other deaths can be survived and converted into a renewed life. This puts very abstractly what this sequence phrases very concretely and often funnily (humour being the form of a kind of resurrection in the face of utmost absurdities—the Human replacing the Divine Comedy); one characteristic mode is that of elegy. Those elegised are poets—Frost and Roethke. At first I could not understand the place of these elegies in the economy of the sequence. Now I see that they relate the quasi-fictional Henry's deaths and resurrections to a reality outside the poetry but which is none the less specially relevant to Berryman as a poet. These poets have successfully made something. They are not merely competing voices, but completed lives—hence inspirational much like Ann Bradstreet, the original American Muse.

Henry's voyage through the dismembered, jagged, desperate and comic cosmos places him in a tradition of other American voyagers of the imagination through reality: the Myself (of "Song of Myself") Crispin (of "Comedian as the Letter C"), Hugh Selwyn Mauberley. In variety of encounter and material Henry most resembles Myself; in formal organisation of experience he is closer to Mauberley. You might see this poem as an attempt to reconcile the two American traditions of the personal-and-national and formal-and-cosmopolitan-traditional epic. Perhaps this is putting too large a strain on the poem. Part of its success is a certain self-deriding modesty, inherent in the lightness of the repeated and basically octosyllabic three eight-line stanzas (a looser, more jagged, elliptical *Don Juan* perhaps: similar in that uncompleteness is not just unfinishedness but part of the content, the celebration of life-energies that leap over gaps). The modesty is also part of a peculiarly modern, urban (rather than urbane) wryness, sometimes blankness. Here the Negro voice is important and completes in a vital way Berryman's verbal picture of man in modern America.

The Songs are very obviously Blues. The organisation of energies has the improvised qualities of slow jazz, its bravura, its domesticity, its loyalty ultimately to basic rhythms. Blues themselves are lamentations, elegies, complaints. They at the same time reconcile, assuage or establish the mood in which stoicism can become an emotional colouration. The Negro voice (I can't make up my mind how well it is done as voice) is of the utmost importance. It adds a new dimension to Berryman's desperation. The Negro is an expert in survival. He is familiar with death and yet somehow continually picks himself off the very floor, clambers out of the very basement of modern civilisation. Supremely a victim, he escapes self-pity through joy in survival. Like the cat, he has nine lives. Henry's search is to learn to be a cat, simply to continue, as coolly as possible, to play it by ear. I'd at least like to believe this is how it works.

the Review No. 15

MARTIN DODSWORTH

MARIANNE MOORE

American society is an open society, at least in the sense that privacy is hard to come by—or so the travellers say. It seems, for example, that you can't put a fence round your garden, so as to avoid your neighbour's glance occasionally, without arousing a general feeling in the community that you must want to do something pretty nasty behind it.

It is all the more surprising, then, that Marianne Moore, who is very American in some ways—for instance, she likes baseball and Eisenhower —should be able to fence her imaginary gardens with such emphasis. The public, of course, is permitted to look round, but not encouraged to do so. Neither the physical appearance nor the tone of her poems is at all inviting. She has marked out her territory in such a way that imitators and rivals are warned off; she has none. Though we may enter her world as readers, we feel that entry is made possible only by the benevolence of a self-denying tolerance on the part of Miss Moore. She insists on good manners and a good education; a visit to her gardens is an occasion for instruction as well as pleasure. We are certainly *not* allowed close enough to see through the dining-room windows, though we have the impression that there is surely something worth seeing there. These familiar objects, laid out in curiously arbitrary patterns, are presented to us with such emphasis by their cultivator that we cannot help feeling that there is more to them than meets the eye—"the power of the visible / is the invisible". There is also a ubiquitous dryness in the soil, which partly explains the sporadic distribution of flora. We stand stupidly amazed in her gardens, her poems opened before us, and are overcome with questions: is there a *rationale* for these extraordinary products? What have we to do with them?

At one level, of course, her poems are very direct. They abound in moralising comment, they have palpable designs on us: "distaste which takes no credit to itself is best", "we prove, we do not explain our birth", "too stern an intellectual emphasis upon this quality or that detracts from one's enjoyment", "inns are not residences". This

straightforward quality of statement is echoed in the apparent scrupu-
lousness with which borrowed phrases are acknowledged: "An
Octopus", for example, quotes extensively from the "Department of
the Interior Rules and Regulations, The National Parks Portfolio",
and favourite sources include the *Expositor's Bible*, Henry James and *The
London Illustrated News*. Miss Moore's love of detail, her insistence on
the accurate use of words, her tendency to give lengthy catalogues of
names and things, her startling ability to detect likenesses in the most
unlikely places, as when she calls a glacier "an octopus / of ice", are
based on an almost childlike respect for the truth. She admires openness
and the ability to act in accordance with one's own nature, without
deviousness. She remarks about the cat Peter:

> To tell the hen: fly over the fence, go in the wrong way in
> your perturba-
> tion—this is life; to do less would be nothing but dishonesty.

The flat directness of her poems is honesty; their idiosyncrasies of style
are the reflection of her nature. To write otherwise would be for her
nothing but dishonesty.

But this account of Marianne Moore's poetry is not in itself sufficient.
Her art embraces contradictory principles. Though she speaks often of
the worth, and indeed necessity, of simplicity, her own style is complex.
The relation between her direct statements is oblique; it is not easily
seen, for example, in lines like these:

> ... *Festina lente*. Be gay
> civilly? How so? "If I do well I am blessed
> whether any bless me or not, and if I do
> ill I am cursed." We watch the moon rise
> on the Susquehanna. In his way
> this most romantic bird flies
> to a more mundane place, the mangrove
> swamp to sleep. He wastes the moon.
> ("The Frigate Pelican")

Furthermore, her poems use rhythm in an *anti*-poetic fashion, to confuse
the reader. His expectations are frustrated by the refusal to set up a
rhythmic norm and by a perpetual use of *enjambement*. When she does
not use free verse, Miss Moore has a preference for intricate stanza-
forms and near-inaudible rhymes, distributed almost at random. Form

is established in order not to be respected. When she is dissatisfied with
a poem in its completed form, she removes passages without any
attempt to patch over the hole left, even when elaborate stanzas are left
hanging in the middle of the page, as in "The Steeple-Jack" or "Nine
Nectarines". "When I Buy Pictures" is an interesting example of Miss
Moore's curious attitude to formal qualities. In *Poems* (1920) it was a
poem of stanzas rhyming *abcbd*: by the time it reached *Selected Poems*
1935 it had been altered in various ways that seem to have forced the
poet to turn it into free verse. At any rate, the result is that the opening
lines, though unchanged verbally, are now quite different formally. I
quote the 1920 text, but indicate the line endings in the revised version:

When I Buy Pictures

or what is closer to the truth, / when I look at
  that of which I may regard myself as the
    imaginary possessor, / I fix upon that which would
  give me pleasure in my average moments: / the satire upon curiosity
    in which no more is discernible / than the intensity of the mood;/

or quite the opposite—the old thing, the mediaeval decorated hat box, / in which there
    are hounds with waists diminishing like the waist of the hour-
      glass / . . .

It is a little disturbing to find that it makes so little real difference which
way the lines are arranged, especially when they once included that
breath-taking *enjambement* "medi- / aeval". One is reminded that
Marianne Moore is a poet who has said of poetry: "I, too, dislike it";
most of her poems suggest a tension between the sort of thing that is
being said and the way of saying it, as though she felt she could not use
another medium than poetry, but rather despised it all the same. There
is a sense of tussle in her best work and a certain messiness in the effect
of her most patterned stanzas.

Now, she is too obviously an intelligent artist for us to put this down
to ineptness in her handling of the form. The sense of messiness, of
expectations frustrated, must be intentional. One way to explain it is
to see it as the expression of personal idiosyncrasy; the sort of thing said
about the cat Peter could suggest this, as a form of behaviour "natural"
to Miss Moore. Such an explanation devalues the poems; it degrades

their style to mannerism and lays a strong emphasis on the whimsical
and fanciful element in the artist. The moral statements are weakened
because they are set in a decorative framework which implies the sort
of aestheticism which they would themselves reject. Miss Moore
praises Hebrew poetry as "prose with a sort of heightened consciousness" and speaks of "the spontaneous unforced passion of the Hebrew
language", but according to this diminished view of her work nothing
seems unforced in it, and "heightened consciousness" is evident only
in the rarefied level of abstraction at which things are dealt with when
the poet is not engaged in that studious attention to small details which
amuses us but scarcely enraptures. To such a reader, the fine description
of Hebrew at the end of "Novices" is made up characteristically of
borrowed phrases, magpie-fashion, and fades away in the manner of
any of her fanciful lists:

> this "ocean of hurrying consonants"
> with its "great livid stains like long slabs of marble",
> its "flashing lances of perpendicular lightning" and "molten fires
>   swallowed up",
> "with foam on its barriers",
> "crashing itself out in one long hiss of spray".

An unfavourable judgement on *this*, though, would surely be setting
too much store by inverted commas. Were it not for them, the lines
would seem unforced and brilliant, a sustained metaphor of depth and
magnificence; if you want to stick by the explanation of Marianne
Moore's style as wilful, if amusing, eccentricity and still admit the
strength of these lines, you must say that they are exceptional in their
direct expressiveness. This places the defender of her poetry in the
position of having to demonstrate that the lines are not exceptional. I
admire Miss Moore's poetry very much; I believe that all her best
poems are simply and directly expressive.

Its subject-matter, though, is neurosis, or rather the neurotic animal
man—

> that tree-trunk without
> roots, accustomed to shout
>   its own thoughts to itself like a shell, maintained intact
>   by who knows what strange pressure of the atmosphere . . .
>   ("Melancthon")

> Not afraid of anything is he,
>   and then goes cowering forth, tread paced to meet an obstacle
> at every step.
>
> ("The Pangolin")

Man is the animal at odds with nature; to describe another animal is to criticise our own life. The cat is an example.

> Profound sleep is
> not with him a fixed illusion. Springing about with froglike ac-
> curacy, emitting jerky cries when taken in the hand, he is himself
>   again; to sit caged by the rungs of a domestic chair would
>   be unprofit-
> able—human. What is the good of hypocrisy?

Miss Moore's interest in the animal world has little to do with the simple parallels drawn with human life in the manner of the Disney film. She is alert to the important differences—expressed wittily here in the use of *unprofitable* which redefines our notion of *profit*, the basis, in its cruder sense, for much that keeps us securely locked within the domestic cage.

She is particularly interested in forms of protection and defence. Man's armour is not neatly built into his organism; it is something that must be acquired by him, like most other skills:

> needing to choose wisely how to use the strength;
>   a paper-maker like the wasp; a tractor of food-stuffs,
> like the ant; spidering a length
>   of web from bluffs
>   above a stream; in fighting, mechanicked
>   like the pangolin.

Her descriptions of other animals make much of their means of self-defence, partly in order to suggest their effortless superiority in this, but also to remind us that the need for it can't be avoided. Marianne Moore's Nature is unfriendly. The jerboa and the salamander offer instruction in the art of survival. The jerboa honours the sand by assuming its colour:

> closed upper paws seeming one with the fur
> in its flight from a danger.

E*

The salamander's protection "was his humility"—

> a formula safer than

> an armourer's: the power of relinquishing
> what one would keep.

("His Shield")

This is the very lesson that has been learnt by the elephant:

> His straight trunk seems to say: when
> what we hoped for came to nothing, we survived.

Now he "expounds the brotherhood / of creatures to man the encroacher".

Man has no humility, cannot blend with the landscape, is always the unhappy exception, clad in armoured complication. In "An Octopus" there is a contrast between the wildness of the natural scene and the tourists who litter it with the signs of their presence, introducing "eagle-traps and snow-shoes / . . . alpenstocks and other toys contrived by those / alive to the advantage of invigorating pleasures". This vandalism has little to do with "what we clumsily call happiness / . . . such power as Adam had and we are still devoid of"."The Greeks liked smoothness" and attempted a kind of conformity with nature in

> resolving with benevolent conclusiveness
> "complexities which still will be complexities
> as long as the world lasts."

Like the mountain which is the subject of the poem, like Henry James, the Greeks are "damned by the public for decorum"—that is, by "a public out of sympathy with neatness". But the poet's cry is:

> Neatness of finish! Neatness of finish!
> Relentless accuracy is the nature of this octopus
> with its capacity for fact.

(The "octopus" is the glacier on the mountain.)

Marianne Moore has learnt her lessons from Nature. Like the jerboa and the salamander, she is modest. She does not express her personality or feelings in poetry. Her extensive use of quotation is part of her modesty; it is also part of her refusal to stand out, to be obtrusive as "man the encroacher" usually is. She forms herself a protective shell from her quotations; they are not her. Then, again, her poems are shells in the sense that feelings are implied, though not actually present. "The Paper Nautilus" cherishes her eggs in a "thin glass shell":

> the intensively
> watched eggs coming from
> the shell free it when they are freed. . . .

In the same way, Miss Moore delicately hints, writing poems can release feelings for her independent of the poetry, yet leaving their marks somehow in lines

> like the lines in the mane of
>   a Parthenon horse,
>   round which the arms had
> wound themselves as if they knew love
>   is the only fortress
>   strong enough to trust to

The feelings most often aroused in her, and themselves giving rise to her eggshell-fine poems, are feelings of distress at the dangerous imprecisions of fellow men. It is not that she is a misanthrope, but that she sees "Life's faulty excellence". She has taken upon herself "The Labours of Hercules", and these include saying

> that it is one thing to change one's mind,
> another to eradicate it—that one keeps on knowing
> "that the Negro is not brutal,
> that the Jew is not greedy,
> that the Oriental is not immoral,
> that the German is not a Hun."

"England" is another poem that attacks such simplified descriptions, even when they are the kind we might view sympathetically: "The sublimated wisdom / of China, Egyptian discernment . . . should one not have stumbled upon it in America, must one imagine / that it is not there? It has never been confined to one locality." It is because poetry has encouraged stock responses of this kind, which blur our vision of the world so that it no longer has "prismatic colour" as it did "when Adam / was alone", that Miss Moore dislikes it. Poetry has excluded "business documents and / school-books" from its subject-matter; she restores them. She is anti-poetic, for the same reasons that she dislikes the tourists in "An Octopus", or the man in "A Grave" who stands in the middle of her view of the sea; poets don't let nature speak for herself either. They blunt our perception by setting up conventional expectations. Miss Moore frustrates those expectations benevolently. She knows that it will hurt, but feels that it is very much a case of kill or cure.

It is for this reason that, although her style is in some ways better suited to free verse ("When I Buy Pictures" is happier in that form, I think), she prefers to use elaborate stanzas whose pattern she flouts almost continually. It is shocking; it may wake us up. But she also uses such complicated forms because, after all, pattern is attractive, and is human. Art is not Nature, but she is drawn to Art too, and some of her most wonderful poems speak of man's ambiguous fortune as artist and craftsman. "Virginia Britannia" broods on the double-edged gift that colonisation was to America; "The Pangolin" praises man, "the prey of fear", who nevertheless

> says to the alternating blaze,
> "Again the sun!
>   anew each day; and new and new and new
>   that comes into and steadies my soul."

"No Swan So Fine", she says, "as the chintz china one", which survives "at ease and tall" though "the king is dead" who reigned over its creation. Art has the doubtful honour of not being fully life, just as man has the ambiguous privilege of not being fully animal. In many ways "Those Various Scalpels" is the best of her poems on this theme, for it brings out perfectly her mixed feelings about us all in contemplating a woman's armoury of elegance, cosmetics and jewels: "Are they weapons or scalpels?" It is a poem at once witty and sad, impressed yet sceptical, quite faultless in the encumbered reluctance of its lines:

> your raised hand
> an ambiguous signature: your cheeks, those rosettes
>   of blood on the stone floors of French chateaux, with
>   regard to which the guides are so affirmative—those regrets
>   of the retoucher on the contemporary stone . . .

The secrecy of Marianne Moore is, then, essential to her art. It is a means both of protecting her own innocent, uncivilised, uncontaminated vision and of making us attend carefully to it. It is a means of presenting us directly with the confusions of Nature, and also the order within Nature; the poet does not intrude a personality. In "Roses Only", which is not included in the *Collected Poems*, she sums up her own attitude to her art:

> What is brilliance, without co-ordination? Guarding the
> infinitesimal pieces of your mind, compelling audience to
> the remark that it is better to be forgotten than to be remembered
>   too violently,
>   your thorns are the best part of you.

The Arctic Ox is important because it is Miss Moore's latest book. In the last twenty years her style has shown an increasing interest in less private forms of communication. Her poems now have an obvious neatness, the tone is brisker and more confident, there is less frustration in store for the reader. Obliquity seems now almost conventional and a little mannered in her work. The opening lines of "Jamestown, 1607–1957" gives a good idea of the later Moore:

> Some in the Godspeed, the Susan C.,
> others in the Discovery,
> found their too earthly paradise.
> Dazzled, the band, with grateful cries
> clutched the soil; then worked upstream,
> safer if landlocked, it would seem;
> to pests and pestilence instead—
> the living outnumbered by the dead.

There is no denying that this new clarity and lightness of touch is pleasing. But without the armoury of style and qualification that we find in her early work a certain sentimentality becomes apparent in her references to nature, and reminiscences of her earlier style appear eccentric as they do not in the *Collected Poems*. We are conscious of a rococo element in, for example, the poem on Yul Brynner's work for the United Nations, which puns "You'll", "Yule", "Yul". But it would be churlish to make too much of this. More to the point, no doubt, is the general consistency of style and purpose which has enabled Miss Moore to reprint slyly here one of the poems from her first book— "You are like the realistic product of an idealistic search for gold at the foot of the rainbow", which is now called "To a Chameleon". She doesn't draw attention to it. Private as ever.

the Review No. 15

FRANCIS HOPE

TOMMY'S TUNES

The legend that the First World War produced a reflowering of English poetry dies hard. It began, I suppose, as one of those exercises in Home Front double-think whereby those not yet killed or wounded were urged to go out and be so, and those ineligible by age or sex for such a distinguished end were persuaded that they too were in some sense involved in an enterprise of high significance. A study of the anthologies which appeared at the time—particularly of their prefaces—reveals some grisly items. E. B. Osborn introduced *The Muse in Arms* (1917) with this sage piece of accountancy: "The youth we have lost in these dread years has not perished in vain; if 'the spring has gone out of the year', as Pericles lamented, yet we are immeasurably the richer for the spirituality they have bequeathed to us, of which the poems in this book are an enduring expression".

Owen and Sassoon originally set out to destroy such rubbish, but their own reputations have become caught up in a similar flame of expiation—anti-militarist rather than patriotic, but still largely a matter of praising their poetry in order to assuage the guilt of not having shared their sufferings. A demotic version, more anti-militarist still, turned up recently in *O, What a Lovely War*: as Ronald Bryden remarked in the *New Statesman*, wars are the culture of the poor. We may have lost a million dead, but we have "If You're Looking for Your Sweetheart" to show for it. (Or, for old-fashioned sentimentalists, "Tipperary".) It's marginally interesting that the introduction to *The Muse in Arms* laments the impossibility of including "real" soldier's songs because the music-hall surrogates had got such a grip (helped by the enfeebling influence of the gramophone) that spontaneous creation was dying out. The view that music-hall and folk-art were identical apparently came later. So did the loving archaeological reconstruction of soldiers' songs in their true, unbowdlerised form. Wartime printed versions such as *Tommy's Tunes* (1916) are not exactly recognisable as Littlewood material.

In any case, much is still expected of the First World War poets, particularly in this commemorative period (which is apparently going to last until November 11th, 1968, at least). Mr. Johnston's essays on them* start from the assumption that they *ought* to have done it well: if Ypres and Passchendaele didn't produce an *Iliad* or a *Battle of Maldon*, there should be good reasons to show for it. He thinks he has solved the mystery, and his sub-title "A Study in the Evolution of Lyric and Narrative Form" anticipates the infuriatingly reiterated solution. The war poets inherited a bad tradition, the Georgian false start. This was a bad tradition by any standards, since it was based on a general outlook of false pastoralism, a week-ender's inability to come to terms with industrial society, and on a linguistic and technical discipline of, more or less, nothing at all. It was also, as a lyrical tradition, unsuited to war poetry, which should be epic, heroic, objectified, positive and narrative. (Echoes of Polonius are not inappropriate to Mr. Johnston's manner.) If the early poets—Brooke and Grenfell—are too shallowly cheerful, Owen, Sassoon and Rosenberg are too shrill, too fragmented, too negative to be counted as great war-poets. Only Herbert Read's *The End of a War* and David Jones's *In Parenthesis* really measure up to Mr. Johnston's formal demands, and only the second—an under-rated masterpiece—really satisfies him.

This is an argument, of a kind, and as an apparatus for rehabilitating David Jones it is both sensible and useful. But if it is to hold up 350 pages, and to act as a measuring-stick for poets as far apart as Rosenberg and Brooke, it involves several supplementary questions which Mr. Johnston never begins to raise. Aren't the problems of a modern epic— any kind of epic—far deeper than those of a garden which the Georgians carelessly neglected? (What comic epics have we had since *Don Juan*, what religious ones since *Paradise Lost*?) And isn't the boot rather on the other foot; isn't the fragmenting experience of the First World War one of the things that has helped to settle the epic's hash (with a few honourable exceptions, like *In Parenthesis*) in this century? Is it really true that the *Iliad* and *The Battle of Maldon*, which are frequently cited as if they had a whole battalion of unnamed isotopes behind them, are the natural models for modern war-literature? Doesn't even nineteenth-century literature suggest that prose, and somewhat dissociated prose at

* *English Poetry of the First World War*. John H. Johnston. O.U.P.

that, is the natural medium of war-literature in an age of *levée en masse*?
(Fabrice on the field of Waterloo is the obvious example here, but *War
and Peace* has some similar scenes.) Doesn't the example of the Thirties
and Forties show that even a strong poetic tradition, used to objectified
and historical themes, may not turn out great poetry even when
confronted by a war—or two wars—far more just and necessary than
the war of 1914? Isn't modern war a classic case of the displacement of
conventional objects (horses, swords, bugles) by things too techno-
logically advanced for emotional or image-making faculties to catch
up with them?

Mr. Johnston does devote a word or two to the last problem, in his
concluding pages, but he hardly bites very deep. He is no doubt a
humane man, and would agree with Yeats that "there is every excuse
for him (Owen) but none for those who like him"—or rather, in Mr.
Johnston's own judgement, for those who don't see his limitations. But
he does sometimes sound as if he is distributing white feathers. First
World War poetry in general is "marked by emotional excess":
Sassoon's "Glory of Women" and "Their Frailty" are "rather im-
moderate and indiscriminatory"; Owen's "achievement does not
measure up to the vast tragic potentialities of his material". Or, as the
Morning Post wrote in a review of *Soldier Poets* (1916), "the poems
which have been twined together are a bright and never-fading rebuke
to the futile and forgotten stuff of 'the half-men with their dirty songs
and dreary'." The introduction to this anthology, once again, excelled:
"the note of pessimism and decadence is absent, together with the
flamboyant and hectic, the morose and the mawkish ... The braver
spirits were shocked into poetry and like the larks are heard between
the roaring of the guns". Their thoughtful handling of universal issues
appears in stanzas like:

> Are we the pawns of a Jevah
> That move on a cross-chequered board?
> Propelled from the back by a lever,
> Controlled, supervised by a Lord?

The point of this juxtaposition is not to make a monkey out of Mr.
Johnston, nor of the bad war-poets, but to show the background against
which Owen and Sassoon, in particular, worked. Mr. Johnston has little
time for other people's indignation.

Unfortunately the phrases "war poetry" and "the war novel" have come to connote literary efforts strenuously devoted to an exposure of the "truth" of modern war, *as if this truth were different from any other kind of truth.*

The italics, and the incredulity, are mine. In another passage he rebukes Owen for the lines

> You shall not hear their mirth:
> You shall not come to think them well content
> By any jest of mine. These men are worth
> Your tears. You are not worth their merriment.

and contrasts this with Blunden's assumption that the reader is sympathetic and understanding ("There are such moments; forgive me that I note them"). It is undoubtedly nicer to be treated in Blunden's way; but I am not sure that it is either more truthful (as I understand truth) or necessarily, in this case, better poetry. There was an abyss between combatants and non-combatants, and Mr. Johnston has implicitly recognised it by excluding from discussion all poetry *about*, but not directly *of*, the war.

Considering his emphasis on heroic models, this is curious: was Homer present at Troy, or Shakespeare (or Drayton) at Agincourt, or Tolstoy at Borodino? The sort of positive, universal poetry which Mr. Johnston's canons demand is more likely to be written by civilians (or after many years' digestion of experience: *In Parenthesis* was published in 1938). Mr. Brian Gardner, in his anthology *Up the Line to Death*, makes the interesting point that Kipling was the poet whom the front-line poets most detested and reacted against, but after his son was killed at Loos he was in a way the closest to them in spirit—much more so than Bridges, Chesterton, Noyes or Masefield. Certainly Kipling's contributions to Mr. Gardner's anthology, as well as those by Yeats, Housman, Hardy and Laurence Binyon, would escape Mr. Johnston's strictures of excessive subjective involvement. There are also some soldier poets whom Mr. Johnston might have taken more notice of (though he has some interesting pages on C. H. Sorley): Graves is an obvious one, and stray poems like Edgell Rickword's "Colonel Cold" or Harold Monro's "Officer's Mess" might bring the lyric partial reprieve.

So might rather more attention to the war itself. "What is the good", wrote Sassoon to Blunden after it was over, "of quarrelling with 1917?" Not much, perhaps, but even Jones admits that *In Parenthesis* could hardly have been written about the war as it was after July 1916. Under these circumstances, Mr. Johnston concedes, "the efforts of the aforementioned poets (Sassoon, Blunden, Rosenberg, Owen) may be viewed with more tolerance; they were indeed dealing with intractable material." He thus concedes, five pages from the end, that his whole argument may have been wrong after all and that Owen really knew what he was talking about when he said that he was not concerned with Poetry. Under the circumstances, "Futility" really is the best one can do—or as good as one can do, since a direct comparison between it and *In Parenthesis* would be nugatory—in writing poetry about the Western Front. Owen's admirers have long believed this; I cannot say Mr. Johnston forces me to change my mind.

It follows from this—again a position that Mr. Johnston contradicts by assertion rather than by argument—that this subject belongs not so much to the history of poetry as to the history of the war. War does not make good poets out of bad ones, though it does frequently make bad poets out of people who wouldn't otherwise have written poetry at all. (Perhaps the initial legend of war fructifying poetry is simply mistaking quantity for quality; in wartime more new poetry is written and more old poetry read.) And the poets involved in the First World War were not the best, perhaps, of their time, though it is always possible that, had they survived, Owen and even Sorley might have been. But as it is, the map read differently. What Pound and Eliot and Yeats had begun before the war they continued after it: a revolution in English poetry that leaves both unreformed and reformed Georgians in the loop of a by-pass. Owen and Jones and Graves are of sufficient stature to endure, but it could hardly be claimed that they influenced many successors, in spite of Day Lewis's tributes to Owen and Cameron's (among others) to Graves. In general they have had admirers rather than imitators. As for the influence of the war on them, it isn't something to be too lightly assumed. Graves and Sassoon were perhaps directed towards concreteness and satire by the circumstances of the war; after it, Graves developed into a considerable poet and Sassoon did not. Blunden—or on a lower level Wilfrid Gibson—appear to have

written before, during and after war with a technical fluency very little
influenced by their subject-matter; and it is the revolution in technique
that now makes their professionalism look thin. It would probably do
the same for Brooke's later work had Brooke survived. Is there any
reason to suppose that four years in the Navy, however much it might
change him in other ways, would modify that initial judgement on
Personae? "Mr. Pound has great talents: when he has passed through
stammering to speech, and when he has more clearly recognised the
nature of poetry, he may be a great poet." Would he be saying anything else of Eliot now?

I don't quite share Professor Davie's opinion that "the legend has to
be symmetrical", that there is no point expecting anything better of
Brooke, or even passing judgements on his verse, since the Augean
stables had not yet been purified; it seems to me that Brooke was both
a bad poet and a bad influence, though not an important one. (Mr.
Johnston, following some remarks of Sorley's, is sharp on "1914".) But
literature is not quite so parasitic on itself as the pure study of "influences" suggests. The problems of a modern language, a modern
poetic form, an imaginative fixing of life in a rapidly changing society,
impinged on contemporary poets more directly because of the war
itself than because of the war poets. In a not altogether rhetorical sense,
all poetry written since 1918 is war poetry; and Yeats and Eliot and
Auden have contributed more to it than Rosenberg or Blunden, or
even than Owen and David Jones. When we read a poem like "Into
Battle"—which is, linguistically as well as emotionally, a more
genuinely "positive" war poem than any of Brooke's—we are struck by
a sense of anthropological distances—as we are at the story that Grenfell
used to go after German snipers in No-Man's-Land, stalking them like
stags and shooting them at point-blank range. It is like reading about
Trobriand Islanders, and yet we know it isn't—hardly a fruitful basis
for any emotive contact. War may still stir secret passions in more
contemporaries than one suspects:

> *Ah Dieu, que la guerre est jolie*
> *Avec ses chants ses longs loisirs*

but hardly fighting itself. Least of all the Western Front, where (although we may be sick of hearing it) a whole generation was slaughtered,

a whole political system uprooted, a whole civilisation traumatised. The problem of turning it into poetry was more than a problem of the appropriate form.

the Review No. 15

COLIN FALCK

ALUN LEWIS

"I want to experience life in as many phases as I'm capable of", Alun Lewis wrote in 1939, a few months before he joined the Army, "—i.e. I'm more a writer than a moralist, I suppose." There can be little doubt that Lewis was a writer: potentially, perhaps, he was the most important writer of his generation in this country. But when he died in 1944 the potential was only beginning to be realised, and a serious judgement of his work and of what he might have gone on to do would probably have to start from the conflict within his character—which he himself only dimly recognised—between the writer and the moralist. The pure talent is inescapable in Lewis's earlier poems, but so too is the moral burden which prevents him from going where he wants to go. Sooner or later in nearly all of Lewis's writing one comes up against a rather Wesleyan, non-conformist psychology, a rather nervous loyalty to democracy, the working classes or Wales, a rather provincial wholesomeness and decency. These things—they are more explicit in his letters*—form a kind of substratum to his work, and it is only in his later short stories, near the end of his life, that this substratum begins to break up and to be worked out in artistic terms.

Lewis went from Wales into the Army and was posted eventually to India and the Burmese jungle. Apart from a spell at Manchester University he never lived in a large city for any length of time. His feeling for nature was always stronger than his grasp of human society, and in his poetry this meant that it was sensible and perhaps inevitable that he should look to poets like Edward Thomas for guidance rather than to the mainstream of the modern tradition. In his prose fiction the result was a certain haziness about social relationships: "my touch isn't at all sure," he once wrote, "my thoughts wander instead of crystallising and I can't imagine the people objectively enough." Many of his stories are rather abstract, and some of them are set in rather standard confrontation-situations like a railway carriage, a hospital ward or an

* A few are published in *In the Green Tree*. Allen & Unwin, 1948.

officers' training unit. But this haziness about the actual goes along with an unusual degree of openness to human possibilities, and at their best Lewis's stories promise something of the universality that we associate with German writers like Mann and Musil.

Lewis has been criticised for allowing himself to be influenced by the Georgians, but it is not always clear what this criticism amounts to. It is true that he was un-curious about verse forms and technique generally, and this may be a good reason for doubting if he would have gone on writing verse for much longer. But where subject-matter is concerned, the urban sophistications of Eliot *et al.* would have been beyond Lewis's range of experience and it is a sign only of his integrity that he did not try to imitate them. What the criticism really bears on, in fact, is Lewis's range of experience. And before being too impressed with it we should perhaps at least ask whether the range of experience of more celebrated and "modern" poets might not also be questioned. How little of nature there sometimes seems to be in the whole post-Baudelairean tradition that modernism grew out of. If more of the Georgians had been good poets, if Lawrence had taken more trouble, perhaps we should now be seeing things differently.

But the criticism has its point. In a poem called "To Edward Thomas", which he wrote while he was garrisoned in Hampshire in 1940, Lewis meditates on Thomas's life and contemplates the view from a hill-top near Thomas's memorial stone. The third part of the poem ends:

> I sat and watched the dusky berried ridge
> Of yew-trees, deepened by oblique dark shafts,
> Throw back the flame of red and gold and russet
> That leapt from beech and ash to birch and chestnut
> Along the downward arc of the hill's shoulder,
> And sunlight with discerning fingers
> Softly explore the distant wooded acres,
> Touching the farmsteads one by one with lightness
> Until it reached the Downs, whose soft green pastures
> Went slanting sea- and skywards to the limits
> Where sight surrenders and the mind alone
> Can find the sheeps' tracks and the grazing.
>
> And for that moment Life appeared
> As gentle as the view I gazed upon.

These lines are nature poetry at its best, and the conclusion itself seems proper to the experience that Lewis is offering us. The softness and gentleness and the veiled hint that even this calm is not perpetual are appropriate and authentic. But three years later, when Lewis has left the English countryside far behind him for the tropical jungle, we still find him speaking of nature in terms of softness and neutrality. He refers to the jungle as a "separate world, remote, unperturbed, indifferent, serene". And although there is a good deal of vivid description in the poem which he actually calls "The Jungle", as well as in the stories which have the jungle for their setting, it is hard to feel that Lewis has really brought the jungle to life for what it is. In a story called "The Raid", the narrator says at one point "You know, I'd have said that valley *hated* us that night"; but the hatred scarcely comes across, and we are more likely to believe him when he speaks of enjoying "the sense of freedom and deep still peace that informs the night out in the tropics". It is significant, perhaps, that some of Lewis's key images of nature at work have a kind of oriental tidiness about them:

> ... the instinctive rightness of the poised
> Pied kingfisher deep darting for a fish.

Nature and the jungle are never really experienced as chaotic or as seriously hostile. We can get a perspective on Lewis here by comparing his view of the jungle with, say, Conrad's; or by comparing his re-actions to India with what Lawrence wrote after a visit to Ceylon:

> The East is not for me—the sensuous spiritual voluptuousness, the curious sensitiveness of the naked people, their black bottomless, hopeless eyes ... altogether the tropics have something of the world before the flood—hot dark mud and the life inherent in it: makes me feel rather sick.

What Lawrence brings to the East is the western tragic vision, the experience of a human world more spiritually advanced—and more alert to the primitive—than the rural Wales that Lewis grew up in. For Lewis nature can still appear as the oriental *tao*, the stream of life: indifferent, perhaps, but never red in tooth and claw. And where Conrad uses the jungle to probe the foundations of liberal democracy, Lewis is too anxious a democrat to be able to follow him. In "The Orange Grove", one of Lewis's most ambitious stories, the officer

Beale is only half-listening when his driver tells the miserable story of his life. Later he begins to think about it: "Hate. Hate. Beale couldn't understand hate . . . But this little rough-head with his soiled hands and bitten nails, his odd blue eyes looking away, his mean bearing, squatting on the floor with kerosene and grease over his denims—he had plenty of hate." It is as though hate belonged only to the socially under-privileged. There is a good deal of Orwell in Alun Lewis—and he sees India very much as Orwell did, in terms of the half-buried conflicts between the native Indians and their alien white rulers. But there is also a mystical side to his nature which Orwell never had. When, at the end of "The Orange Grove", Beale hands over his driver's dead body to the benevolent care of a band of gypsies it is as though his journey into the jungle—the artist's journey into the interior—was all the time only a version of the religious pursuit of grace or *nirvana*. (Though realism, it is worth noticing, demanded that the gypsies should be paid five rupees for their services, and it is never quite clear what they are going to do with the body anyway.)

The problem of writer *v.* moralist—i.e. the problem of how far, if at all, the writer should allow his creative intuition to be modified by what his moral conscience tells him is right—appeared to Lewis only in disguise. It appeared, as it has to many poets from the early Romantics to Rilke, as the problem of art *v.* life. His mystical inclinations seemed to point towards art and withdrawal; his moral convictions pointed to life and a commitment to humanity. Lewis's art is a long way from the pure pursuit of illumination which the Symbolists at their most ivory-towered professed to believe in: on the contrary it is marked at every turn by moral incursions of one kind or another. His poetry, especially, is fragmentary and uneven for this reason. But while his realistic instincts (because that, surely, is what it really was) prevented him from going very far towards pure symbolism, a part of him was always drawn to the aesthetic ideal: as Ian Hamilton says in his introduction to his selection of Lewis's work,★ Lewis "seems always, haltingly, to envisage a Platonic universe that lives behind the perishable real world, and to seek as his central reward those intense moments in experience when a harmony between the two worlds is attained". And for his life

★ *Alun Lewis: Selected Poetry and Prose.* Edited and with an Introduction by Ian Hamilton. Allen & Unwin, 1966.

itself the conflict of art *v.* life was central. How can, how should, the artist live with other people? From his earliest stories to his very last Lewis circles around the question of the artist's isolation: much of the time he seems to feel, or fear, that the ordinary people, the soldiers, the professional officers, are doing his living for him. His leaning towards withdrawal and contemplation explains the appeal which the oriental temperament had for him, and makes it easier to understand his sense of revelation, just after he arrived in India, when he came upon a little statue of Buddha somewhere in the hills "Silently and eternally simply Being, / Bidding me come alone." And yet this was the same man who in more worldly and western tones altogether had said "I want to experience life in as many phases as I'm capable of." These tensions are very clear in Lewis's letters, where he seems deeply committed to and at the same time strangely distanced from his wife and his family. The place where he seems to have experienced the strain most intensely was in his conception of love. Love, in Lewis's poems and stories, is curiously unreal and abstract: there is an idealism about it which seems not to have been put to the test of any very concrete experience. Phrases like "the holy mystery / Of boy and girl together / Timelessly" have a breathless sincerity about them, but they appear in the poems as stop-signs to the probing intelligence, limits to areas of experience rather than areas of experience themselves. And in the few poems where love is actually given a concrete embodiment it tends to come over as a rather ordinary kind of domesticity. In "Dawn on the East Coast" the soldier's momentary vision before he is killed is of "A girl laying his table with a white cloth". It is the right vision for the poem, perhaps, but we also tend to assume that the soldier is not Lewis himself; and Lewis gives us no better idea elsewhere of what his own vision might be like. The exception to this general criticism is the poem "Goodbye", where the lovers are very soon to be separated:

> Tonight remains, to pack and fix on labels
> And make an end of lying down together.
>
> I put a final shilling in the gas,
> And watch you slip your dress below your knees
> And lie so still I hear your rustling comb
> Modulate the autumn in the trees.

And all the countless things I shall remember
Lay mummy-cloths of silence round my head;
I fill the carafe with a drink of water;
You say "We paid a guinea for this bed,"

And then, "We'll leave some gas, a little warmth
For the next resident, and these dry flowers,"
And turn your face away, afraid to speak
The big word, that Eternity is ours.

This is very genuine, but it throws a strange light on "the holy
mystery / Of boy and girl together / Timelessly". Where and how is
this mystery to be consummated?—unless in separation. One feels, in
the end, that Lewis's idealisation of love was something that would
have had to give way, to be broken down and reconstructed; and one
suspects that he had begun to realise this himself. In his letters, as in his
poetry, love and war are always contrasted, and usually in an obvious
and even sentimental way: he allows himself no hint that there might
be affinities between the two. But one can sense the pressures building
up, the doubts growing as to whether the ideal of spiritual love could
ever be realised in the kind of ordinary life that he might return to when
the war was over. Something of Lewis's confusion appears in his poem
"To Rilke", which refers to the experience of finding the Buddha (or
Vishnu) statue, and ends:

Then I fell ill and restless.
Sweating and febrile all one burning week,
I hungered for the silence you acquired
And *envied* you, as though it were a gift
Presented on a birthday to the lucky.
For that which IS I thought you need not seek.
. . .
The jackals howl and whimper in the nullah,
The goat-herd sleeps upon a straw-piled bed,
And I know that in this it does not matter
Where one may be or what fate lies ahead.

And Vishnu, carved by some rude pious hand,
Lies by a heap of stones, demanding nothing
But the simplicity that she and I
Discovered in a way you'd understand
Once and forever, Rilke, but in Oh a distant land.

Another strange poem—a strange love poem particularly—and Rilke might have had a good deal to say about it. But the poet is without any doubt trying to have things too many ways at once. There were two worries which Lewis never quite distinguished in his own mind: first, whether the artist could ever really belong to life; secondly, whether an ideal love could ever be realised in the flesh. But both of them drew him away from the ordinary ideas about life and love which he tried simultaneously to affirm.

It was only in his last years that the real pattern behind these conflicts began to declare itself and that Lewis began to deal with them in an unmystified way. His real instinct was to be a writer: the statement which he made to this effect in 1939 was truer than he can have realised when he made it. It was not morality or democracy which bound him to the real world and held him back from Buddhist escapism: it was the true writer's instinct to experience life in all its phases. When he asked to be sent into action, Lewis said characteristically that it was "loyalty to the Welsh soldiers" that motivated him. But he also said "They seem to have some secret knowledge that I want and will never find out until I go into action with them." We can trace this urge towards experience even in Lewis's earlier work: in his story about an air raid, "They Came", for example, where there is a strong sexual under-current which is never satisfactorily resolved in the story itself and which makes the ending, with its noble affirmation—"My life belongs to the world, I will do what I can"—seem just a little hollow and over-dedicated. Later these things become more explicit. In "Ward 'O' 3 (b)" it is the sexual charisma of Captain Brownlow-Grace which really dominates the story; the other characters, and not least the sensitive Lieutenant Weston, scarcely come to life by comparison. In "The Orange Grove" Staff-Captain Beale dreams "of a Bombay whore whose red kiss he still had not washed from his arm, allowing her to enter where she would and push into oblivion the few things that were possible to him in the war and the peace." Sexual experience is not the only thing that haunts the background of Lewis's work, but it plays a large and comprehensible part. When his wife chided him for the number of sexual references in his writing, Lewis's answer in his next letter was ". . . breasts, breasts, breasts, you roar in a splendid Presbyterian rage. Well, unfortunately, the world is full of breasts. I can't help it any more than you can. And where there are human beings there's sex. And I just write how I see things—and I see a lot more sex than I ever write." Not sexual at all, but equally subversive of the morality which operates on its surface, is the Nietzschean under-current in the story "Almost a Gentleman". On the face of it the story is at the expense of the officer class who "found out" that the Jewish cadet Burton was not really officer material; but the question on which the story closes, ". . . how did they know that he had the soul of an underdog?", has a Lawrentian edge to it which suggests that Lewis himself agreed with them. Lilies that fester, Lewis comes near to saying; but his democracy gets in the way—and not surprisingly when he is writing about an institution so dependent on corrupt distinctions as the British Army.

If he had followed the course towards which these instincts were leading him, Lewis would have had to choose between his moral convictions and his art. Or rather, he would have had to assign them each to their proper sphere. And certain questions might have appeared in a new light, or disappeared altogether. The part of him which wanted to get away from life and contemplate might have resolved itself into the part of him that was simply avoiding life and the part of him that quite legitimately wanted to find the necessary peace and quiet in which to work. (There is nothing like the Army for accentuating the conflict between art and life.) We should not suppose, though, that Lewis's democratic faith would have wavered in real life, whatever might have happened to it in his art; and in this he could have taken us a step beyond the great generation of the moderns. But his personal relationships, and his loyalty to his Welsh origins, would certainly have come under a severer strain than he had allowed them to experience: there is a hint of this, perhaps, in his decision shortly before he died that he would not write any more letters to his parents for some time.

Supposing, though, that these were the problems that confronted Lewis, just how clearly did he come to see them? Were there perhaps other conflicts of which he has left us little or no trace? Almost anything that we decide seems to be based on too little evidence. Above all, the circumstances of Lewis's death are still uncertain. If, as seems likely, he committed suicide, why did he do so at that particular time and place, so shortly before he went into action? It is possible, whatever in fact happened, to detect a suicidal streak in many of the things that Lewis said and wrote (as one always can, perhaps, in those who are strongly drawn towards contemplation and denial of the world). Was Lewis still worried about whether he could bring himself to kill?—as he had been when his principles first led him towards enlistment in the Army in 1939. Was he in despair about the state of the world? Or did he simply see no way of going on, when the war was finally over, with the life that he had left behind him? Or was his death really, as the Army court of enquiry said it was, accidental?

If he had gone on writing, and had stuck to verse, Lewis might have given a new depth to modernism by rooting it back in the nature from which it has become alienated. Unlike some of his contemporaries, he was never content with success on the level of style alone—and for this reason he has been called a "late developer". There is an utter truthfulness about his work and an unusual degree of intellectual distinction. Poems like "All Day it has Rained" and "The Public Gardens" deserve a place in almost any modern anthology. But it seems unlikely that Lewis would have made his break-through in verse. Many of his best lines are lost in unsatisfactory poems—for example:

> And summer leaves her green reflective woods
> To glitter momently on peaks of madness.

Or:

> I who am agonised by thought
> And war and love
> Grow calm again
> With watching
> The flash and play of finches
> Who are as beautiful
> And indifferent to me
> As England is, this Spring morning.

Or:

> Only the fleeting sunlight in the forest,
> And dragonflies' blue flicker on quiet pools
> Will perpetuate our vision
>
> Who die young.

Or:

> Gulls lift thin horny legs and step
> Fastidiously among the rusted mines.

And few of even his best lines have the inevitability which would suggest that Lewis might have quarried away at them, generated more of them, shed the heavy load of discursive reasoning and made himself into a lyric poet in the manner of, perhaps, the Rilke of *Neue Gedichte*. What seems more likely is that he would have become a novelist. The reflection and debate which found their way into his poems were better suited to prose fiction, and his intellect was too powerful and open and wide-ranging for him to be able to accept a system—as Yeats and Eliot did—and confine himself to verse. Above all, his interest in experience was too strong for him to be able to confine it easily within the limits that the modern lyric imposes. His prose, on the other hand, has the elements of greatness; that is to say, by studying Lewis's actual work in the light of his psychology and his philosophy of life—so far as we can yet understand them—we can see that he had laid the foundations of a major achievement. His stories, though sometimes sketchy and inconclusive (and always very short), are unmistakably ambitious. But everything is potential, hardly anything is realised. That is why it is so important to search out what he did not tell us and to try to understand what he did not understand himself. Hamilton's otherwise very sensitive introduction ends rather lamely when he tries to draw us away from speculation about Lewis's death and says that it is enough that "we have the poems and stories from which this volume is selected. They tell us what Lewis wanted us to know." They do; but it is not enough. More could be, and needs to be, said about the problems that Lewis faced: they are the problems that face the modern artist still, and it is one measure of Lewis's importance that he found them arising in his own life and began to look for an honest way out. Hamilton's selection includes Lewis's best and most finished work, and this is something to be grateful for when a writer so good has been so neglected for so long. But behind the work there is the life which seemed to promise so much more—and which could still tell us so much more if we had the material and the means to understand it.

the Review No. 17

JOHN FULLER

RANDALL JARRELL

The caprices of transatlantic publishing kept Randall Jarrell from us too long. His poetry did not appear in book form in this country until 1956, and now he is sadly dead, killed in 1965 in a traffic accident. There seems to have been hardly time to assess his stature; our obsession with his contemporaries (he was born in 1914, the same year as Berryman, three years before Lowell) is complete. It is true that our knowledge of most American poets follows the same pattern of delay, but Jarrell did not have the idiosyncrasies to demand the current attentions of our journalists. His personality was already before us, of course, in such notable essays as "The Obscurity of the Poet" from *Poetry and the Age*, in his novel *Pictures from an Institution*, and in such familiar anthology pieces as "La Belle au Bois Dormant" (about a murder victim in the left luggage) or "The Death of the Ball Turret Gunner". These striking poems set a standard of shock and laconic pity which the *Selected Poems*, as they were bound to do, seemed at one blow to dissipate: if only we could have known the four earlier collections as they had come out.

His poetry sprang fully-armed from the best American soil. He was hard on his first book (*Blood for a Stranger*, 1942) when he came to compile the *Selected Poems*, but it is clear that the initial influences were to persist, that the Frostean speaking tone or the slightly crypto-Fugitive fastidiousness have always been there. One could have wished for more oddity, more direct myth. When, in that first book, he begins a parable:

> The Sheep is blind; a passing Owl,
> A surgeon of some local skill,
> Has undertaken, for a fee,
> The cure ...

the interest aroused relates, I think, to the Ransom of "Captain Carpenter" rather than to the Ransom of "Janet Waking"; but the point is that the reverse is most usually true. That is to say that Jarrell's aim was that of a sympathetic understanding of the persona or situation presented, rather than the dynamic verbal enlivenment of it. Above all he wanted to be clear. Take, for instance, his early developed interest in the disturbing psychological implications of fairy tales (the manner, perhaps, of the Allen Tate of "The Robber Bridegroom"). One of the best of these is "A Quilt Pattern" (from *The Seven League Crutches*, 1951) in which a little boy is dreaming as his mother tip-toes outside the door:

> ... "You are full now, mouse—
> Look, I have warmed the oven, kneaded the dough:
> Creep in—ah, it is warm!—
> Quick, we can slip the bread in now," says the house.
> He whispers, "I do not know
> How I am to do it."

The poem retains its dramatic life, but forfeits much to the textbook revelation of infantile sexuality (a comparison with Graves's "The Bed Post" may show what I mean). Jarrell wielded a narrator's glee, even his compulsion; but the sense of discovery or of risk was often blunted by the omnipresent intellect.

Indeed, one feels, what a properly ambitious and intellectual poet Jarrell was! The latest volume* (one hopes he left more poems) shows his virtues in miniature. Here is that rare sense of effects hard worked for, and actually achieved; of a frontal but flexible assault on themes seen to be demanding; of the assumption of poetic duties and poetic craft, tempered all the while with the warmth necessary to breathe life into the statue. Here was a poet whose wit saluted his tenderness, and whose tenderness returned the salute.

He was good in the monologue form, and good at understanding women: in combination ("Seele im Raum", "The Woman at the Washington Zoo") these skills showed him at his most memorable. There are poems in *The Lost World* like this ("Next Day", "In Nature there is neither Right nor Left nor Wrong") with the usual well-plotted analysis of femininity from behind the leapt barriers of the monologue, but the two longest and best poems about women are "Hope" and "Women", both from the male point of view. The first of these, a Christmas meditation on the ascendancy of the female, has

* *The Lost World*. Randall Jarrell. Eyre & Spottiswoode, 1966.

a persuasively sad sustained humour in Jarrell's most dextrously free
style:

> Sometimes, watching on television
> My favourite serial, *A Sad
> Heart at the Supermarket:
> The Story of the Woman Who Had Everything,*
> I look at my wife—
> And see her; and remember, always with the same surprise,
> "Why, you are beautiful." And beauty is a good,
> It makes us desire it. When, sometimes, I see this desire
> In some wife's eyes, some husband's eyes,
> I think of the God-Fish in a nightmare
> I had once: like giants in brown space suits
> But like fish, also, they went upright through the streets
> And were useless to struggle with, but, struggled with,
> Showed me a story that, they said, was the story
> Of the Sleeping Beauty. It was the old story
> But ended differently: when the Prince kissed her on the lips,
> She wiped her lips
> And with a little *moue*—in the dream, a little mouse—
> Turned over and went back to sleep.
> I woke, and went to tell my wife the story;
> And had she not resembled
> My mother as she slept, I had done it.

The wit is often very consciously plotted like this, and Jarrell's own
voice is frequently there, a ghostly raconteur (in another poem, a
woman choosing cereals with names like *Joy* and *All* finds herself
quoting William James: I'm sure she isn't meant to seem so solemn
about it). But then, the narrative sense does lend poise to what might
be quite bald discoveries, as here in "Woman":

> Men's share of grace, of all that can make bearable,
> Lovable almost, the apparition, Man
> Has fallen to you. Erect, extraordinary
> As a polar bear on roller skates, he passes
> On into the Eternal . . .
> From your pedestal you watch
> Admiringly, when you remember to.

The reader is misled by what looks like fastidiousness in those first lines.
The pointing of the remainder is pure Jarrell, especially with the hint
of his characteristic aposiopesis. To generalise, but to remain dramatic;

F

he does this not by great verbal invention (the cartoon image is make-shift) but by remaining in sure control of the tone, in a way that Frost would have approved when he said "The ear does it". The effects on the page are simple, but the voice is everything—

> When you first introduced me to your nurse
> I thought: "She's like your wife." I mean, I thought:
> "She's like your nurse—" it was your wife.

Jarrell's judgements of people (here of "A Well-to-do Invalid") are sympathetic because the mental process of making a judgement is accurately realised in the voice. Even if one obscurely feels that it needn't be true (say, that the rich are unhappy) the notion is achieved, it is a perception, not doctrinaire ("Hope", "Three Bills"). By contrast, he is far less interesting on himself. The title poem (and one or two related pieces) is about his childhood in California. This material is elaborately and evocatively presented in splendidly unobtrusive terza rima, but the sentiment (of the relished but essentially empty mirror-image of nostalgia) is supported only by detail out of some *New Yorker* indul-gence. These poems carry far less impact than the briefer pieces that Jarrell throws off with apparent ease, "In Montecito" for instance, a semi-anecdotal mystery with a Chandleresque setting, or this poem "Well Water":

> What a girl called "the dailiness of life"
> (Adding an errand to your errand. Saying
> "Since you're up . . ." Making you a means to
> A means to a means to) is well water
> Pumped from an old well at the bottom of the world.
> The pump you pump the water from is rusty
> And hard to move and absurd, a squirrel-wheel
> A sick squirrel turns slowly, through the sunny
> Inexorable hours. And yet sometimes
> The wheel turns of its own weight, the rusty
> Pump pumps over your sweating face the clear
> Water, cold, so cold! you cup your hands
> And gulp from them the dailiness of life.

A clue to Jarrell's fallibility lies in a word like "inexorable", but how effortless, organic and accurate the conception of this poem seems. You have to take its sentiment, as you have to take an even more blatant sentiment like that of the mother's memories in "The Lost Children", in good faith. Far from being a liability, this quality is turned to good account in much of Jarrell's poetry, in "To a Girl in a Library" for instance, once you have abstracted from it that tone of patient half-affectionate comic incredulity that the poem shares with some of the brilliant (and savage) cultural essays in *A Sad Heart at the Supermarket*. There is a kind of aggrieved innocence in the celebrated war poems, too, that yields the stunned and fairly unhelpful repetition of the supposedly explanatory "These are. Are what? Are" ("Transient Barracks") or "It happens as it does because it does" ("Siegfried") or "Still, this is how it's done" ("Eighth Air Force"). Here Jarrell could not supply an answer, but the war poems above all will last: this is because even where he seems to be almost too blank (or, more frequently, too intimate) to chart the morality of war with the necessary precision, he does quite clearly perceive how he can deal with his subject in terms of images and language. Sometimes the diction is a little strained, but it seems now a period touch. The war poems show a public hell, an individual dream, in imaginative and concrete equations. A good example is the opening of "Eighth Air Force", exact, moving, metrically assured (providing such a perfect context to the despairing/laconic phrase I have just quoted from it):

> If, in an odd angle of the hutment,
> A puppy laps the water from a can
> Of flowers, and the drunk sergeant shaving
> Whistles O *Paradiso*! shall I say that man
> Is not as men have said: a wolf to man?
>
> The other murderers troop in yawning;
> Three of them play Pitch, one sleeps, and one
> Lies counting missions, lies there sweating
> Till even his heart beats: One. One; One.
> O *murderers*! . . . Still, this is how it's done:
>
> This is a war. . . .

There is no denying that Jarrell becomes sententious, even biblical, in the remainder of the poem, though the poem is not (could hardly be) spoiled thereby. Jarrell is like this: his poetry has groped for no epiphanies, created no symbols, forged no new language; and he is a poet who often seems vulnerable and tentative without, strangely enough, losing that particular kind of fertile authority that he shares with a poet like MacNeice. This authority is fully in evidence in *The Lost World*: the supple sensibility, sharpened by wit, sense and humane concern, will be much missed.

the Review No. 16

CONVERSATIONS

A NEW AESTHETICISM?
A. ALVAREZ TALKS TO
DONALD DAVIE

ALVAREZ: You wrote recently an article called "Towards a New Aestheticism". I thought it was a very moving piece of prose but I wasn't quite sure in what direction it was moving. I wonder if you would like to explain yourself just a little bit.

DAVIE: Yes, well I hoped it would be moving towards a new aestheticism, since that is what I called it. I'm not really very serious about that, I don't think, but it does seem to me that some of the topics that interest me most in respect of poetry today are blocked because of a built-in prejudice against aestheticism and Art for Art's sake and Walter Pater. It so happens that for some years now I have been able to set my ideas in order about the poems I write and the poems of other people by thinking in terms of analogies between the different arts—how is poetry like music? How is poetry like sculpture? Now I don't argue that this is the one right and proper way to talk about poetry or that this gives you a truer version of poetry than any other. But the climate of literary opinion being what it is I seem to find that people won't even let me begin to talk this way. For this whole way of talking and thinking . . .

ALVAREZ: I take it that you, at one point or another, came to the conclusion that poetry was an answer in itself and it seems to me that what you are trying to say in this idea of "Towards a New Aestheticism" is that there is no further answer other than the ones you can get in poetry, and the more self-enclosed poetry can be the more likely it is to be effective. Let me tell you a story. When I was an undergraduate at Oxford, an American—who shall be nameless—arrived in Oxford and went around saying 'Poetry is the most important thing in the world and one must be professional about it'. Well now, in the face of the kind of 'frou-frou' that passed as a literary life in Oxford at that time this was marvellous. It seemed to me that I wanted to stand on the chairs and cheer. It seemed to me something very good, and almost rather brave to say. Well, I've seen the chap more or less ever since—less more recently. When I went to America about five years later, I found him ravaging around on the literary-political scene, with a wife and two kids, and an ice-box as big as Verlaine's garret, still saying that poetry is the most important thing in the world. It seemed ludicrous. He had simply never grown up. Now you don't mean that.

DAVIE: You've never heard me say that.

ALVAREZ: But you know what I mean. Are you implying that in this idea of a new aestheticism? What is your new aestheticism? Is it simply Walter Pater, or what is it?

DAVIE: No, I said in that article that what I call the new aestheticism is seeing poetry and all the arts—but poetry, since that is the one we are concerned with—in terms of the relation between the man who makes it and the medium which he uses. This—it seems to me—is what was valuable about Walter Pater and that climate of opinion. It seems to me a relation which is now no longer, or very seldom, considered n our talk about poetry.

ALVAREZ: Your implication in the article was that the only relationship which is considered now is the relationship between the man and his society rather than his medium. Well, now I agree with you that this is inadequate too; although I think it is less inadequate than you do. What I'm not sure about is to what extent you want to consider poetry as a relation between the man and his medium and to what extent you want to consider it simply in relation to the medium itself—to the medium concerned with itself.

DAVIE: This comes back to your earlier point which I didn't understand and still don't understand about "poetry is the answer". I ask: "the answer to what?"

ALVAREZ: Well, the answer to all one's anxieties and tensions and the general mess one has to come to terms with in life . . .

DAVIE: Yes, well of course it isn't the answer for anyone, but in so far as one is a poet (and this, I suppose, is where the professionalism comes in), this is the particular answer that one is concerned with. It seems to me unnecessary, and I should think you'd agree with me, unnecessary and wrong—if this is the job you've taken on, and it's very difficult after all to write good poems—to be worrying all the time about the other answers which can be given in quite different terms from the ones you happen to have chosen. We all have our jobs to do.

ALVAREZ: But the point is that the job is a more complicated and responsible one than simply being a skilful writer. It's the job of living in society and being, as it were, a responsible grown up human being, isn't it? And something that says that the man must be sacrificed to the poem, to the discipline of art, seems to me nonsense, and seems, in a sense, a kind of childishness. To move smack into your domain: there is a kind of double talk that goes on apropos Ezra Pound—where can you separate Pound the craftsman from Pound the political juvenile delinquent? Now, he is a very good test case for he happens to have written some very beautiful poems—when he can forget about everything except poetry; he is very sensitive to language. But his grownupness, his professionalism, functions on no other level, and as he is always bringing other levels into his poetry I think this is really debilitating.

DAVIE: Yes. Of course, I don't agree with this view of Pound. Here, oddly enough, it is I who am maintaining, as far as I see it, that technique and technical expertise cannot do as much as you claim that it can. You claim that sheer technical expertise in Pound, sheer feeling for the medium of language, can produce beautiful poems. This I would deny, you see.

ALVAREZ: I think he has produced some very beautiful poems but they are all about literature. And I don't just mean "Mauberley"; I mean the early Cantos, the first seven Cantos anyway; I mean "Propertius", where it's feeling for the literature of the past, for literary experience of the past. I mean, there he is, from Idaho—and suddenly literature looms into his life. He has all the reactions of a man from Idaho, except this fantastic enthusiasm and skill and ear, and sheer pleasure in using his ability—on that one subject. He reacts to literary occasions.

DAVIE: I still maintain that with all the skill, with all the delicate ear, with all the pleasure you take in sheer verbal manipulation you do not in this way get good poetry. A good poem is necessarily a response to a human situation. "Propertius", for example. "Propertius" is a response to the British Empire at a certain point of its decline, and all the literary manipulation is there deployed for that specific purpose; to register what it was like to be an American poet living in England at a time when he saw the British Empire tottering to its fall. Or so it seems to me.

ALVAREZ: I see this. But what is also in Pound is not just the pleasure in manipulation—I put that badly—I mean also this involvement with literature, this passion for literature, which is very much a whole passion, in which all his intelligence comes to work.

DAVIE: Well now, perhaps I can come half-way to meet you here, because I would certainly want to maintain very firmly that a man who has this sort of feeling for literature and for a literary use of language can, while operating upon that material, in fact transcend the limitations which he has in other circumstances. That is to say a man who is emotionally immature can, by dint of the passion which he has for literature, transcend his emotional immaturity for the sake of the poem which he is making. If you are going to say this is what Pound does, then I would be near to agreeing with you.

ALVAREZ: I think he does when he is writing well: but I think he only does when he is writing on literature—that's the tragedy of Pound— well, not on literature, but with some kind of literary occasion behind him; when it's a translation, or a reminiscence of classical myth, or something like that.

DAVIE: But why is this a tragedy? This is the way in which the body of achieved literature helps us now.

ALVAREZ: It's a tragedy because one feels that the occasions when you can do this are very rare. The occasions with Pound became rarer— because of the time he was living in—as his political involvements got more urgent. As a result there is a great mass of his writing which is plainly so much below the standard of what he could do.

DAVIE: Well, this is true, no doubt. Perhaps we had better face up quite frontally to this business of Pound's politics, which of course I deplore as much as you do. But don't you see, it seems to me that by and large the English are right not to trust poets and artists when they set themselves up as political sages and pundits. If you tick over on your fingers the political pronouncements of those whom we would agree to be the great poets of the past century, they are nearly all politically remarkably unreliable people; and if when you are asking that a poet should be responsible, you ask that he also be politically responsible then it seems to me you are asking for too much.

ALVAREZ: What you're really trying to say is that by some curious chemistry nearly all of the really important writers of our time, in fact of all times since Shelley anyway, have been on the Right, haven't they? It is almost impossible now for a good poet to be on the Right—since the rise and fall of the Third Reich. What do you get? You get Betjeman.

DAVIE: Yes. Yes. Still, all the same, I wouldn't accept your position on that, it is impossible for a good poet to be on the right even in this country. I don't think that the history of poetry over the last hundred years gives you any sort of basis at all for the sort of correlation that you are making between political standpoint and poetic achievement. Poets in general do not have political good sense. That's all I'm saying.

ALVAREZ: No, but I think politics is the key issue, because I think that we are living in a kind of society where it is absolutely impossible to avoid them. The facts of history are too much. It's not a question of your having to adopt what Leavis called "cocktail party communism" or anything like that, as they did in the Thirties. It's something much more urgent. You can't just opt out of society like that, because you're in it for better or for worse, and no-one is going to fight your battles for you.

DAVIE: This I agree with, and I'm not in the least arguing that the poet should leave politics alone. In fact ,the poems that I'm writing now are semi-political poems. But I wouldn't be able to write them if I felt that a peculiar responsibility was involved for me to be more sensible in the political conclusions I reached than the next man in the street.

ALVAREZ: No, I do agree with you there. But if I had an aesthetic myself—which I suppose I don't—it would be that phrase of Eliot's

F*

which I've worked to death: "The only method is to be very intelligent." I think if one goes around in the cloak-and-dagger of the intellectual, one should at least try to live up to it. It's very important to be as intelligent as one can, as tough-minded.

DAVIE: Yes, indeed. I would hope that in the political poems I write, the political issues I discuss are discussed, I hope, with more intelligence and at a deeper level of feeling and with more multifarious human connections, and all that . . . I think that the quality of the exploration is important. It seems to me not different in fact from the position in respect of ethics too. Leavis and Leavisites are right to demand from writers an unusual degree and quality of moral concern. This is quite a different matter from supposing that the conclusions they come up with will be the right ones.

ALVAREZ: One's own training has been so much involved with Leavis—though he'd be the last person to want to have to claim any of us—nevertheless it seems to me the Leavisite position is no longer wholly tenable because the kind of concern that is involved depends on standards which seem no longer totally relevant in our present society.

DAVIE: Yes, I would agree.

ALVAREZ: Pottel, the Marxist critic in Leeds, or Sheffield, is it . . .?

DAVIE: You mean Kettle, actually.

ALVAREZ: Kettle, yes that's right. Not Pottel's Miscellany, Kettle's Miscellany. Kettle has said that the real trouble with Leavis is that he never came emotionally to recognise that the Industrial Revolution has taken place. This is presumably why there is this huge stress on Lawrence: because Lawrence, in a sense, has roots in pre-industrial revolution England, and wanted—and the older he grew the more exacerbated he grew, as in, you know, Lady Chat.—wanted to return to a world which hadn't been touched by the Industrial Revolution. And in the "Leavisite"—as distinct from Leavis who is very much more intelligent—this becomes a vague invocation of the Wheelwright's Shop and all the rest of the romanticised pre-industrial country. This is nothing to do with our society now. What I would like to do is to get my own position clear; and it is this: twice in the last few months I've been to

Auschwitz—and if one had any kind of reaction—well it's a very difficult thing to cope with, as you know, but it gives one a new scale of values. There is a poem by Marianne Moore "On Poetry" which begins "I, too, dislike it. There are things that are important beyond all this fiddle." It seems to me that what happened in Auschwitz, and the other 130 concentration camps that there were within the Reich, and that's happening in concentration camps in Russia and presumably in China and so on, is of an order that makes it very very important to, as it were, be sane about one's own identity, to be sure about one's own identity, because the whole movement of the concentration camps is the movement to destroy individuals, and towards the kind of efficiency that destroys art. One has simply got to say that the seeds of the concentration camps are in us all—we've all got these self-destructive tendencies, tendencies to give up, not to give up the fight, but simply to hand over your identity. And you can do it in all sorts of ways; you can do it in your personal life, you can do it in your working life. But to use the immortal words of E. E. Cummings: "There is some shit I will not eat." This is absolutely vital. One has got to be able to cope with one's society—its traps and shams. And one's aesthetics, as you call them, must follow that.

DAVIE: Well, they do more than follow that, they are that. We must be careful not to agree too much. I agree with everything you say and as far as I'm concerned the blank sheet on which I try to write my poems is precisely the battlefield on which I maintain my identity. I find it and maintain it.

ALVAREZ: No, I think we don't really agree, because my feeling is that you would say that the medium is the thing by which you discover your identity, that the medium is the thing on which one imposes or fights out one's identity.

DAVIE: Yes, this is a real difference between us. It seems to me you see the self that one is as something given that one has to fight through the barrier of language on to the paper. For me, I could cite authorities . . .

ALVAREZ: Something given but at the same time in itself revealing—it's not given, it's not known, it's not worked out beforehand. I don't mean that at all.

DAVIE: Well, yes, this means you are nearer to what I would maintain which is that a dialogue ensues between the self that you are and the medium you are operating with. And what comes out of the marriage between—if you are lucky—the marriage between the self that you are or thought you were and the medium that you are operating with is the self that you truly are, you are finding your self in the process of writing the poem.

ALVAREZ: You are talking about your poetry. Let me do the same. When I went to Auschwitz, it was the most traumatic experience I've ever been through. Even now, it's still appalling. I tried to write a poem about it. I picked up the poem a couple of months later and it started changing, but it didn't come out. I recently drafted some kind of version, and completed it. There is no Auschwitz in it at all. There's nothing about the concentration camps at all. It has become a personal poem about loss. It does seem to me that the self-revealing nature of, you know, "What is the experience?" "How do I cope with it?" goes into the machinery of the self, sure, but it comes out quite different from what you'd expect. Where I think we differ is that I think one has to face that there is a great ugliness, and pain in the nature of all our experience. It's very difficult to go into the ivory tower. I think fundamentally my basic criticism of your attitude towards aestheticism is that—you know—you've got it easy because you are in Cambridge. I'll take this up though, in a moment. What one has to do is to get a language which is tough enough and clear enough, and pure enough. Not tough in an Allen Ginsberg way, but in a sort of unflinching way, in a facing what there is way, in facing what you don't want to have to recognise, which is done superbly by a poet, like, say, Robert Lowell who seems to me very much the best poet now writing. You create this language of the self, and it's a language very disciplined, highly disciplined, and it's got to be because one has not only got to write of oneself, one has also got to be intelligent about it.

DAVIE: Yes, well what I always feel in conversations like this, because this is not the first one we have had, is that in fact we do agree most of the time about the poems that we like. It's only when we try to find reasons that the different vocabularies we use make us seem to disagree, which is odd. I agree for instance that Lowell's poems from *Life Studies* onwards represent the best model in the English language that I know of—of poets roughly of our generation or my generation. All of this I would agree with. It was, oddly enough, in order to explain to myself what I saw as the remarkable distinction of—for instance—Lowell's poem "To the Union Dead" that I found myself going into something that interests me very much—I mentioned it earlier—this business of the analogy there is between poetry and the other arts. It was in relation to that poem that it seemed to me that I understood for the first time something of what is meant by poetry becoming like music. Now this is just my way of explaining to myself the distinction which I feel, the impression which it makes on me. The impression is the same in your case, I'm convinced, but you find a totally different vocabulary for it.

ALVAREZ: I think it's rather more than that. One of the bones of contention there has been between us a good deal is the poetry of Charles Tomlinson which I do not admire nearly as much as you, although I think actually his most recent poems—since his book—show a marked improvement. New depth and all this. You tend, aren't I right, to admire poetry which is concerned with the other arts. I tend to admire poetry which is concerned with, . . . well . . . let me explain: Sydney Nolan was with me when I was last in Poland. As we drove away from Auschwitz his comment was: "It's a bastard being human." You feel when you see the conditions—I'm sorry to come back to this but it's very much on my mind—you see that it would not only be better to be dead than to live like this but that it would be infinitely better to be dead. Then you go into the chimney, the incinerator . . . well . . . it's not simple . . . It really is a bastard being human. It seems to me that what one has to cope with in poetry—as I wrote in the introduction to this Penguin anthology, in which I refer to the "new seriousness"—is the ability to express the complexity, the bastardy of being human and having to face all the pain and . . . remain sane . . .

DAVIE: Well, I'm entirely with you in this sense of urgency. I haven't been to Auschwitz, I haven't had an experience quite as traumatic as that, but I think I know what you mean—as you know I've been to Eastern Europe. I felt very much the same as you. But to come back to Tomlinson. What you find suspicious in the admiration I have for Tomlinson's poems is that so many of them are about the other arts.

These aren't, in fact, the poems which I admire most and the difference to me is that Tomlinson's are as often as not poems about things. What you are asking for is poems about people—all the time. The only reality which you really think of as adequate for poetry is the human reality, the social reality, the psychological reality. That is to say, the reality of the sort of person I am and the sort of person you are and the sort of relationship there is between us. I agree that this is very important. Tomlinson most of the time is talking about the sort of reality which there is in him, the sort of reality that there is in that stone wall, the relation that is set up between him and that stone wall. Now I quite see that this might very well seem to be a less urgent concern than the ones which you prefer. My way of getting round this—and it's more than a way of getting round, it's what I profoundly feel, would go something like this: I daresay that you would agree that the cardinal rule in human relations is for one partner in the relation to respect the integrity of the other person, not to attempt to violate it, not to attempt to dominate it, not to attempt to possess. Well, we've been hearing this from Lawrence and many others for quite a long time. We ask "how do we learn to do this, how do we learn not to dominate, not to be aggressive?" Simply a resolution: "I will not dominate", is not good enough. And it seems to me that the sort of thing which Tomlinson in certain poems in a sense recommends—realising this stone wall as different from all other stone walls—in its otherness, its thusness, its quiddity. To see things in this way, to see a tree thus, to see a stone wall thus, affords a sort of model which you can then apply to human relations.

ALVAREZ: Let me take up this image of the stone wall because it seems to be very useful. I think fundamentally the difference is this: all sensitive people nowadays are in the same boat. In the same ghastly position. We are all standing there with our hands against this stone wall against which there presses on the other side, a flood tide of neurosis, both inner and social. What you are saying is "If I keep my hands hard against it and look away or look at the detail of the brick, this is the answer." What I am saying is "Christ, it's hurting my arms." You see the difference? We've all got to deal with the same things. It's going to break down and flood us if we are not damn careful. I don't think this is just a personal paranoia—I think this is the general social situation. That's why, I take it, people sit down in Trafalgar Square. You are saying: "We're here and I'm making the effort, but while I'm making it I might as well describe to you the construction of the wall that is keeping us safe." I am saying: "Look at the difficulty of the situation which we are in."

DAVIE: No, it seems to me something like this. I agree with you that humanity and human relations are under an intolerable strain in our time. An all but intolerable strain. We are all at breaking point. Neurosis is very prevalent indeed and menaces all of us. Now, in such a situation, the principal first requirement is to keep sane, to keep the neurosis at bay as far as possible . . .

ALVAREZ: Not just to keep it at bay but to learn to know what it is. So you can live despite it. So you can cope with it.

DAVIE: Yes, all right. Well . . .

ALVAREZ: There's no need to be so defensive about it, is what I mean.

DAVIE: Well . . .

ALVAREZ: I think that is where we really differ . . .

DAVIE: I think perhaps it is where we differ. I would say that if human relations are under the intolerable and perhaps unprecedented strain they are under today, one must make what efforts one can to relieve this pressure so that human relations may as far as possible be decent. One does this certainly not by burdening the human relation with all the enormous weight of anxiety and responsibility which it seems to me you want to put upon it.

ALVAREZ: Let me put it in a very vulgar way. I think the difference is that, what you are saying is that "My affair with X was a terrible bloody mistake—not necessarily a mistake—a terrible bloody failure, and brought nothing but pain on us both. So the hell to it. I will, as it were, be content merely with masturbation." My feeling is that "It was a terrible failure but here I go again into exactly the same kind of affair with someone else which will be even worse." But, that's it. That's what I meant by defence, I suppose.

DAVIE: Of course, I refuse the masturbation analogy. Surely the world is full of people who've got themselves into the wrong sort of relationship, which is, all right, a bloody awful mistake for them both.

ALVAREZ: I don't believe in mistakes . . .

DAVIE: All right then, a failure. But what do they do? Generally what people do is learn to live with it. They make the relationship somehow more viable by taking a lot of the weight off it, by not expecting as much out of that relationship as first they did, by seeing it as part of a much wider pattern of disseminated interests.

ALVAREZ: There is probably a difference in years here. You were in the war, whereas I was a kid in the war. This makes a slight difference. It seems to me a lot of marriages now go straight on the rocks because of a feeling that there is no time to live with a failure. One has to make something of one's life—there's probably not much time. There is that kind of neurosis underneath it now. I think that having come through the war, you've got some slightly larger frame of reference. I'm very pro the frame of reference. But let me again quote Nolan, who has a theory that art doesn't actually mirror the times, but acts as a kind of Early Warning System, and that what you get in art now you are going to get in society in ten, twenty years' time. As it were, the kind of contempt for the human being which one had in Cubism is mirrored in Auschwitz. Auschwitz is full of straight lines. It's very efficient. The good poets today, in America say—let's get on to neutral territory—the one's I admire—people like Lowell and Berryman—whom I think we both admire, are poets who are writing about violent neurotic breakdown. Where the English poet used to go on the bottle, the Americans now go into the mental homes. It's a kind of occupational disease for a poet. I think this could be the kind of society we are heading for. If we are heading for a nuclear war it's going to be a bloody great breakdown.

DAVIE: Well if we are heading for that . . .

ALVAREZ: The thing is to try to cope with these forces and create real poetry out of them. Not just express them as, say, Ginsberg did in that poem "Kaddish", which seems to me a rather heavily edited transcript of what happened between Ginsberg and his psychiatrist when he got on the subject of his mother.

DAVIE: What I find hard to take here is the assumption that poetry lives or falls with society. We all know that if there is a nuclear holocaust, everybody's killed so there are no poets; but I really think that poetry can survive a social breakdown and, we had to come to this sooner or later—I think both of us are more or less infidel, more or less agnostic, more or less unbelieving people.

ALVAREZ: I'm an atheist.

DAVIE: I think, honestly, your being that, and my being pretty much that, is what leads us naturally to suppose that the only grounds for poetry are therapeutic and social. Of course, in the history of poetry down the centuries, however much it may embarrass us in fact, the grounds for poetry have frequently been religious or—this is a new word I've lately learned (I'm not quite sure what it means)—ontological. It does seem to me increasingly—though it's embarrassing for me to admit it because of my own agnosticism—we may be selling the pass on poetry from the start when we don't allow that it may have metaphysical or religious sanctions. This is what I meant by respecting the otherness, the being of a tree, a stone wall, a landscape. Even if there were a complete social breakdown there would still be a poet with a tree in front of him, a poet with a stone wall in front of him.

ALVAREZ: Now look, that's a terrible piece of emotional muddle. I remember once when I was about fourteen or fifteen and I was busy discovering literature, and trying to write appallingly bad poems—I read some article, I can't remember where—maybe I heard it on the BBC or maybe I read it in some ghastly paper—where a lady writer, of course, said that, you know "we are all poets: anyone who has stood in front of a beautiful landscape and felt sort of moved by the landscape is a poet even though he can't say it." Well, that's rubbish. I don't believe that there are any specifically poetic emotions to be released by a landscape. There's a fundamental difference here. I, as you know, climb mountains, but I can't stand mountain landscape. It bores me starry-eyed.

DAVIE: This seems to me very instructive. The man who climbs mountains in order to conquer them is of course not the man who respects them for what they are in themselves.

ALVAREZ: This is your aestheticism, fundamentally, isn't it? Or is your aestheticism concerned with language, the nature of the medium? The nature of the contemplation or the nature of the medium, that's what I really want to know.

DAVIE: My aestheticism is designed as purely a short-term manoeuvre to try to rehabilitate a notion of aestheticism, the notion that poetry is an art simply in order to break what I see as the constricting climate of opinion in this country, by which you can only talk about poetry and justify poetry in social, ethical terms. This seems to me the easiest way of getting back to realising that possibly it is just as reasonable to talk about poetry in metaphysical and religious terms.

ALVAREZ: You have a very limited interpretation of the word "art". At the end of your article, for instance, you say—you are talking about the difference between art and life and so on and about these young students of yours who would sooner, you say, read Valéry's poems than Lawrence's, Charles Tomlinson's sooner than Philip Larkin's or Ted Hughes's—now I think this is restricting yourself—although I myself am a great admirer, an enormous admirer of Valéry. But I think there is also considerable art and skill and subtlety in Lawrence's poems when they are good. There is the ability to create objects, so that they're not only out there but they're in here, too.

DAVIE: Lawrence really fits my case extraordinarily well. That famous anthology piece of Lawrence's, "Snake", gives me precisely what I'm asking for. The response of the human to the non-human, splendidly rendered. It seems to me that it is—as I understand it—your programme for poetry rather than mine which would tend to exclude such poems and look on them as necessarily trivial because they are not essentially human, not dealing with human relations.

ALVAREZ: To go back to the written word, I praised "Snake" very highly. I think it is very much one of his best poems, but—as you must know—I don't take what you call the "New Left" line. I don't criticise poetry according to the class it comes from. It seems to me, though, that you can really criticise a poet like Christopher Logue simply because of his almost Fascist fascination with power. The real point that no one has made about Christopher Logue is that something like "The

Lily White Boys" might easily have been written, not by Brecht, but
by the young Goebbels.

DAVIE: Yes.

ALVAREZ: It seems to me that one should do social analysis of that kind
in poetry, but when there is something being said, and where something
very original is being done to the language, as with Lawrence, when he
is writing well, and as Ted Hughes seems to me to be doing, then I
think you have got to break down this distinction which you have
made, I think, rather than I, between Art and Life.

DAVIE: But the distinction between art and life is broken down every
time one writes a poem. One is forced to talk in these terms because
these are the terms that are current . . .

ALVAREZ: Now I think this is where you fail to rise to the—what do
they call it—the challenge? You had this idea once of "The Poet in the
Imaginary Museum". Now, I think really what my objection to your
idea of aestheticism is—when we talk about it there is very little difference between us—when you actually get down to it, you take what is
fundamentally an extremely academic point of view; that is, that there
are styles which have been created in the past, they can be more or less
tarted up for our use now, but they are there and they can only be
expanded. Now it seems to me that really new things are happening all
the time which have their roots in the past, but they grow a long way
from their roots like some—to use that thing I once told you not to
write poems about—like some cypress tree. The top is a long way from
the bottom.

DAVIE: If in my broadcasts on the Imaginary Museum, I said what you
impute me to say now, I now unsay it. I do not believe there is a repertoire of styles from the past which can, as you say, be tarted up . . .

ALVAREZ: What you are saying is, let's get back to Pater, let's get back
to Valéry, and my thing is "let's get forward to something new". I
think this is what, say, Robert Lowell has done.

DAVIE: Let's get forward from them to the next thing. Let's not write
off our past.

ALVAREZ: Well, let's get back to Charles Tomlinson, who is obviously a serious poet, but about whom we disagree. At the end of Charles Tomlinson's book was a series of poems very closely modelled on early Pound and Eliot—the Laforgue things. Now, there was a review by Hugh Kenner which seemed to be absolutely disingenuous, where he said that English poets have never coped with American poetry, and Tomlinson is the first man to do so, ergo he is the first really good English poet. This seems so stupid. The point is, these poets were writing in 1917. Charles Tomlinson was doing it forty years later at least. Times have changed.

DAVIE: But what's wrong with that argument is precisely the ergo. In fact, you find yourself saying something very near to precisely this in the introduction to your new Penguin Anthology. I was interested to see that you are there, as I think very rightly, lambasting us for our insularity—and this I think is true. We got our peep into Europe and the rest of the world through the work of these two American expatriates, Eliot and Pound, and the Irishman Yeats, and—as you put it in the preface to your anthology—what we have done ever since has been to get our heads back again as quickly as we can to this private island paradise of ours. You analyse, very interestingly and to my mind very justly, the three "negative feed-backs" as you put it, which have enabled us to do this. This analysis of literary history is precisely mine and I don't understand why you don't draw the same conclusions from it as I do. Let's go back then, to them, and go forward from there.

ALVAREZ: You have only read half my introduction, or three quarters of it. What I actually go on to say is that people have gone on from there. People like Lowell and Berryman, the two I quote—they take for granted that a poet doesn't have to be some blindly inspired seer, some Sitwellian fiddler with words or what have you, but he's got to be intelligent and he has got to be very skilful. He has also got to face the fact that he is moved, whether he likes it or not by forces which are very difficult and very destructive. He has to face this in his poetry, and—you know, in England we didn't have any Forties—the Forties were fundamentally the final giving up of all this Eliot stringency and so on, in the face of beer-swilling wartime neurosis. We don't have to go back as far as Eliot or Pound. If you need models there are models.

There are a lot of people in their forties writing in America. The thing is to go on from there.

DAVIE: Well, all right. This I agree with. Let us go back to Lowell.

ALVAREZ: Let us, for Christ's sake, face the fact that we live in a pretty complicated thing called Europe and not just a rather less complicated thing called the British Isles.

DAVIE: I entirely agree with your view of the importance of Lowell. And let me remind you—you of all people—that Lowell is a very Poundian poet. He has just published a book of translations, you too have helped to publish his translations of Villon in a newspaper—he is very thoroughly in this Eliot–Pound lineage.

ALVAREZ: He is infinitely better than Pound. I think his translations are better, very much more personal. There is not, in fact, this simply literary involvement. His involvement is so much deeper. His personality is showing so much more. Pound keeps his hemline down.

DAVIE: Yes, indeed, that's perfectly true. It's a matter of Lowell's intention. His intentions are Poundian at any rate. I agree that he doesn't perform as a poetic translator in anything like as good a way as Pound does.

ALVAREZ: Well, well, well . . . as they say in Westerns—prove it. I think the Lowell "Villon" is better than the Pound "Propertius". And I'm an enormous admirer of Pound's "Propertius".

DAVIE: On this then we would differ. But this isn't the central issue. Can I at this stage, as I warned you I would—quote you something?

ALVAREZ: Yes, please do.

DAVIE: This is from Pasternak's "Dr. Zhivago" and Pasternak at this point is talking about Zhivago's experience when writing a poem. I quote: "After two or three stanzas, and several images, by which he was himself astonished, his work took possession of him and he experienced the approach of what is called inspiration. At such moments the correlation of forces controlling the artist is, as it were, stood on its head. The ascendancy is no longer with the artist or the state of mind which he is trying to express, but with language, his instrument of expression.

Language, the home and dwelling of beauty and meaning, itself begins to think and speak for man and turns wholly into music, not in the sense of outward audible sounds but by virtue of the power and momentum of its inward flow." Well, that is enough. What I would ask about this, is it a mere gaud of rather windy rhetoric or is it, bearing in mind that it is Pasternak writing it, in fact saying something significant and useful about the act of poetic composition? My point in asking the question is simply that our vocabulary, I believe, prevents us from even beginning to understand what it is that Pasternak may here be saying.

ALVAREZ: I don't agree with you. I should have thought actually that the vocabulary and the concepts he is using are those of the nineteenth century. What he is saying is true. I am sure he is right. One's own experience—in a very much more paltry way, when you and I write, or try to write, poems, bears this out. But the actual way in which it is put is wrong. It's the Aeolian harp thesis all over again, isn't it? It seems to me that nowadays, somehow or other, we know too much. It's very difficult simply when writing about it, not actually writing, but writing about it later, simply to accept this blindness of inspiration; and the whole attempt when writing poetry, when manipulating language, is to understand what is going on as you do it. At no point can you give up the ghost, throw up your hands and say, as Edith Sitwell used to say, "It's all a question of those dark vowels."

DAVIE: I read this not at all for the sake of the inspiration but rather for the sake of the sentence where he says "the ascendancy is no longer with the artist but with language, his instrument of expression" and still more "language itself begins to think and turns wholly into music." Now both of these it seems to me are experiences which I can, in the way you have talked about it, partially confirm from my own experience in writing poems. As you point out, the vocabulary which they use is nineteenth century vocabulary. It is—let's face it—the vocabulary of Walter Pater and aestheticism. It is only Pater and his disciples who were the last people to talk of language in poetry turning into music. You know perfectly well that in the give and take of literary talk in this country, as it might be between you and me—I can't even use a phrase like "the music of poetry" or "poetry aspiring to the condition of music".

ALVAREZ: It's like using the phrase "magic", isn't it? The old school mistress line.

DAVIE: Well, precisely. Nonetheless this is talking about a reality which I know and which I think you know and we are absurdly prevented from talking about it simply because the vocabulary which is available for us has been smeared, tainted by association with a man who died sixty or seventy years ago.

ALVAREZ: We won't have to dig his skeleton out of the cupboard, it seems to me. I think, really, I know what the difference is now between us. Let's take Zbigniew Herbert, the Polish poet, whom we both agree is absolutely first-rate—in what he does and in the way he does it. He is a poet who is very much on his own. He lives in a Marxist society and will have no truck with the Marxist tools of translation of experience. He does it very independently but is infinitely a political poet. What I think you have here—when there is this great pressure—unlike most Poles he wasn't in the concentration camps but had a very rough time indeed in the Partisan army; he saw too much too early, if you like— what one has is a kind of insistence on the facts of society, on the hard, resistant things there, so to speak. Things impinging on him as a man moving in society. This kind of factuality is what makes his poetry good and at the same time very involved, committed. He has this ability to re-create rather abstract states of mind, but in terms of these facts all the time. There's something terribly hard about it. This un- yieldingness seems to me so much more worthwhile than talking about a stone wall. In *Encounter* last summer there was a very beautiful poem of his called "Fortinbras's Elegy", which is Fortinbras talking about Hamlet. It is the elegy of the political man on the non-political man, the man who couldn't stand the pace. It's marvellous . . . clever, ironic . . . and in it the whole of modern Poland, and the whole of Hamlet seems to be. It does seem to me that he faces the facts; and the facts in Poland are terrible. We don't know what the war was about. When you go over there you realise we had nothing in this country.

DAVIE: I think it is no accident that we find ourselves talking about poets of Eastern Europe. What strikes me about these poets from Eastern European countries is that, having been brought face to face with the agonies of the human condition in our time, this does not make them in the least embarrassed about talking about Art with a capital A, talking about poetry becoming music. This was from *Doctor Zhivago*—here was an Eastern European writer who was certainly brought face to face with the brutalities and atrocities of what the human condition is in the present century. It is only we who have this bad conscience and we have it precisely because we haven't experienced it, and we imagine what it must have been like to be a Pole or a Russian or a Hungarian. As far as I can see, among the acquaintances I made in these countries, it has the effect which is, I should have thought—inspiring, of confirming them more than ever in their values, in the value of the poetic act, of the act of the imagination. They speak with all the less embarrassment, all the more confidence about the creativity of the human imagination, about its indestructibility, its inexhaustibility . . .

ALVAREZ: I grant that they are very much concerned with aesthetic matters but it seems to me their aestheticism works on a much more serious level. They are not concerned with the minor irritations that plague us, like manners in poetry and so on. They are concerned with getting the poem as perfect as they can, in itself, and at the same time, with making it as inclusive as it can be. After all, if poetry is to continue to be worth the effort in the present time, it must be a concentration of experience, not a diffusion of it.

the Review No. 1

WILLIAM EMPSON IN CONVERSATION WITH CHRISTOPHER RICKS

RICKS: I think the obvious first question for anybody who likes and believes your poems as much as I do is why there haven't been many of them lately.

EMPSON: Well, it wasn't a rule. I just found in Peking I was writing some and it struck me they were bad, I didn't want to print them. I hope that when I'm made to retire, I'll be able to start writing again. If you look at the collected edition of a nineteenth-century poet, you'll find that the middle bit is frightfully bad—he begins well and he often gets all right again at the end, but all that long middle bit you might just as well leave out, I think. When I found I didn't want to print, I said O.K., I'll leave it alone. The motives which made me want to write had I suppose largely disappeared. I didn't feel I had to do it, anyway. I think many people actually feel they've got to go on, because it's the only way they can support their wife and children or something, and it very often happens with poets that they have this haunting feeling that they are given magical powers which are suddenly taken away from them. Well, they'd very much better stop writing poetry and do something else, I think.

RICKS: What do you think are the motives that will reappear when you retire? What will be different then?

EMPSON: Well, merely that you wouldn't feel so distracted by practical things that have to be done. The capacity to reflect about life can reappear. The old often do feel more sympathetic to the young than the middle-aged because the middle-aged have got to earn the money, after all.

RICKS: Have you kept copies of the poems you haven't printed?

EMPSON: I haven't destroyed the copies; they may be lying about.

RICKS: Because a friend of mine has found out about this play which made you very famous at Cambridge.

EMPSON: That I'm sure was destroyed. It wasn't very good anyway. But I tried quite a lot to write plays. The failed plays were lying around in quite a quantity for some time. I don't know whether they're still in a drawer, so to speak. Turning out the drawers will be an occupation for my old age, except that I shall have to find some means of earning money for my wife and children. The retirement is awfully important in the modern academic world; it keeps them much more sane to think that at the age of sixty-five all this is going to stop. I'll have to be purged and renewed.

RICKS: One thing struck me about your long-playing record: the way in which you left out "Arachne", although everybody has kept on about it. I've always felt that "Arachne" presents your interest in life's contradictions more crudely and unsympathetically than some of the other poems. What do you think about that poem?

EMPSON: I left it out because I'd come to think that it was in rather bad taste. It's boy being afraid of girl, as usual, but it's boy being too rude to girl. I thought it had rather a nasty feeling, that's why I left it out.

RICKS: Do you read all the things about yourself? Have you read *La Poesia di William Empson* by Morelli? It's the only book on your poems.

EMPSON: No. I've agreed to have a selection translated into Italian. It's very odd, that. The Italians are very energetic, of course. There's a translation of *Seven Types of Ambiguity* appearing in Italian now. I had a long correspondence with the author, who pointed out a great deal of nonsense in it. It was rather a severe correspondence. I scolded him back for not understanding the high bogs and the mountains, but he wiped my eye a good deal.

RICKS: A similar thing from the record was that you played down both "This Last Pain" and "The Teasers", though these are the poems which I think the people who have written well about you, like Wain and Fraser and Alvarez, offer a lot of space to. What exactly is your disagreement with the current view of these? Ought I to remind you of your note on "This Last Pain"?

EMPSON: Somebody told me it was like Oscar Wilde saying that you ought to wear a mask and then you'll grow into your mask. This seemed to me positively embarrassing. I didn't want to be like Oscar Wilde in this business of being affected, and I couldn't see why it was different. I felt uneasy about it. I do feel it's writing, as it were, to a theory without my being quite sure what the theory comes to, or what it means or something. I felt rather doubtful whether it meant anything very sensible. I do think it's pretty. I like it for the singing line quality. But it seemed to me I was writing up a subject which I hadn't thought through. That was why I felt shy about it.

RICKS: At the end there is very good formulation of your general thing about not rushing to these hateful available extremes by which we either know what we're doing and then we burn people, or we don't know what we're doing and then we're indifferent when people are shot. I thought it got over that difficulty. It's a poem which is always in my mind, as explaining to people how one can behave without believing in these awful absolutes and on the other hand without not believing in them.

EMPSON: Yes, you express it very sympathetically. I feel that kind of thing quite seriously. I'm sure that's O.K. But then when I'm suddenly told it's exactly like Oscar Wilde, being affected and so on, and ... though a most worthy man and very able, kind and helpful and so on, the thought of behaving like Oscar Wilde does get under my skin. It means being affected all the time. That's not what I'd want it to say. So, in a sense, I've never come to terms with the poem again somehow.

RICKS: What about "The Teasers", then?

EMPSON: Well, I wrote a lot more of it, and it started grousing and grumbling about the conditions of the modern world, and then I thought this is disagreeable, I don't like what I'm saying, and so I cut it down to rags so that it doesn't make sense, you can't find out what it's about. Of course, these powerful minds in the business of criticism, they're fascinated by something that doesn't make sense; but they can't make out what was in the cut verses because it was something quite irrelevant.

RICKS: You think it's all not true, what they say about it?

EMPSON: When dear old George Fraser says it was all against being horrified by women when they're menstruating, and offering my person to all the women in the world and so forth, I was much shocked. I don't entertain these shocking sentiments at all, do you see? Absolutely nothing to do with what was in my mind; I wouldn't even have thought it was in George's mind. No, I'm afraid that the business of guessing what it means when there isn't enough evidence to tell the answer is one we've all trained ourselves in. I just cut out the bits I thought were in bad taste and it didn't leave enough to make any sense really. That's what happened to "The Teasers". But a beautiful metrical invention, I do say. I wish I'd been able to go on with it because it sings so; but that was what happened, I could only give this cut version.

RICKS: Are there any ways in which you feel that people have misconstrued or been positively unhelpful?

EMPSON: I don't quite think that. When I was young, Dr. Leavis praised me very much; although I do insist I was getting published already. The idea that I've never repaid him properly is, it seems to me, unnecessary. But still, he praised my first volume and then, when the second one came out, he swung away and said it was a failure of nerve, it showed that Empson had become too cowardly to write good poetry. Twenty years later you'll find this copied out exactly by the Leavis disciples. Well, he was quite right, I think, to feel that he'd overpraised Empson before—that was what was really going on in his mind, perhaps. But the idea that Empson lost his nerve with the second volume has always seemed to me very unreasonable. The first book, you see, is about the young man feeling frightened, frightened of women, frightened of jobs, frightened of everything, not knowing what he could possibly do. The second book is all about politics, saying we're going to have this Second World War and we mustn't get too frightened about it. Well, dear me, if you call the first brave and the second cowardly it seems to me that you haven't the faintest idea of what the poems are about. And so I do get irritated when I see these disciples of Dr. Leavis still repeating that the second volume showed a failure of nerve. You may say it's a failure of nerve to stop writing altogether, but I don't know that I think that. It wasn't a failure of nerve to write *The Gathering Storm*: I still say that.

RICKS: I think it's poems like "Aubade" and "Reflection from Rochester" which run most in my mind, but it's true that they are very much harder to talk about, aren't they? We know where we are with all that Donne/Metaphysical line, we talk about your calm and your poise and so on, whereas the late ones are pretty difficult to criticise.

EMPSON: Well, they were meant to be plain good sense, what everyone was feeling about the occasion; they're meant to be very much about the political situation. "Aubade" is about the sexual situation. When I was in Japan, from 1931 to 1934, it was usual for the old hand in the English colony to warn the young man: don't you go and marry a Japanese because we're going to be at war with Japan within ten years; you'll have awful trouble if you marry a Japanese, and this is what the poem is about. But, of course, the critic—as it is so far away and so long ago—simply doesn't know that's what it's about.

RICKS: Yes, but it does get difficult all the same. At the end of "Aubade" I can see what it's about, but I'd find it very difficult to translate into French.

EMPSON: Well, I suppose it chiefly meant that you can't get away from this world war if it's going to happen, and that it isn't any use thinking you can go to the South Sea Islands—lots of people got awfully caught by thinking they could get right away to the South Sea Islands—the very centre of the more important parts of the war. London was a good deal quieter. It just says, "All right, we can't marry, we must expect to separate." But it's the last verse you're thinking of. I just thought there ought to be more in it to claim the puzzle was larger. It's a kind of passive endurance. We have to put up with it, we can't avoid this situation of history. It's pretty flat, I should have thought. I can tell you why people make revolutions: they feel a conflict and they don't know what they expect, and they make a revolution merely because they get so irritated. It seemed the best thing in this case to leave the house; and I would leave Japan after my three years. It seems sensible to do something about it, whereas in fact you can do nothing about it, so eventually the country will have to resist. Surely that's enough for it to mean, isn't it? Owing to your beautiful sympathy and your expecting it to be good, you thought it meant something wiser.

RICKS: Why I think it's so good is that the two refrains are quite incompatible in the first two-thirds of the poem. Now, at the end, they start to swap over in a curious sort of way, and start to merge into quite a different attitude: it seems to me that it's about, on the one hand, the tragic principle of integrity and dignity and so on, and also about a comic principle, of decency and comfort. Why I think it's so good—"it seemed the best thing to be up and go"—is because it doesn't—as everyone now thinks—insist that looking after oneself, or not going mad, is terribly ignoble. The danger of the tragic principle is of one kind of soulishness by which this other principle comes to be thought of as mere expediency.

EMPSON: You get a good deal of Chadbandism now, that's quite true, yes. If I was moralising now, like most middle-aged men in most periods, I would moralise in rather a low-minded way. That's a good reason for not writing poetry at my time of life. I sympathise with what you say. But after all, if you're saying that the conflict is between "the heart of standing is you cannot fly" and "it seemed the best thing to be up and go"—if you are an Englishman with the right attachments living in Japan, you could leave Japan and go back to England, where you might resist the forces of evil, the invader. Surely that would do if you want an absolutely flat solution of the two refrains. One is to go away from Japan and the other is to stay in England.

RICKS: Yes, I agree it makes very good literal sense, and I think it's a good story. But I also meant that it insisted that there are two principles and that they are *both*, in certain circumstances, equally desirable and as good as each other. It's like your note in *Essays on Criticism* about saints: that some people object to saints on the grounds that there is another moral principle which is not saintly at all; it's not that saints have the moral principles and that other people are rather desperately expedient—it does seem to me that the poem widens out to be about this kind of thing. All these things that Hugh Kenner doesn't like about you: when he quotes your remark about life not being a matter of understanding things but of maintaining one's defences and equilibrium and living as well as one can, and that not only maiden aunts have to do that—he thinks that's very like a cockroach, and disagreeable.

EMPSON: I'm glad I haven't read Hugh Kenner.

RICKS: So you picked upon him as an adversary by the merest chance in *Milton's God*?

EMPSON: No. He wrote wickedly about other matters. If he wrote wickedly about me it is pure accident.

RICKS: But, of course, he's terribly clever. He's very good on Alice, and how important Alice is for you.

EMPSON: Well, when I say he's wicked, what I mean is I disagree with his fundamental attitude. He's more neo-Christian than any other neo-Christian, I think. A very able man, but with a mistaken hold of wrong principles. But what he said about my poetry was very incidental to that. But I'm delighted with your thinking of the two refrains of "Aubade" corresponding to the two legs which we must all stand on— one of them heroism and the other reasonable good sense; it never occurred to me. Of course, they're meant to be a slight contrast. But I never piled so much dignity on to the story.

RICKS: I think "Let it Go" is good because, where everybody else is saying it's our duty to go mad, and be Christ, and take the whole burden of the world on our shoulders, and so on—what you say is that it's our duty not to go mad, but, on the contrary, rather quietly to try and make things better.

EMPSON: There I think your kind heart is putting too much into it. I'm saying what lots of people would have said in prose. I just happened to put it into six rhyming lines.

RICKS: But it's very difficult to put the case for not going mad in a way that doesn't sound just complacent and uncaring. It's a very eerie poem, isn't it? That "whole thing there" at the end is like a maniac on the Tube, fixing one with his eye and threatening these terrible things. You think it's a cheerful poem, do you?

EMPSON: I certainly don't want to present myself as the wise old Toby: I'm as liable to go mad as the next man. I'd certainly insist that it's rather lucky I preserved my sanity. I don't deny that the prospects of horror are always fairly large.

RICKS: What do you feel about the influence you're supposed to have had on the poets of the Fifties?

EMPSON: Well, honestly, I don't like much of it. But it's largely because

I'm an old buffer: the point has been reached where it is unusual for new poetry to seem very good to me. I haven't liked it very much; but I haven't liked any poetry, whether it's supposed to be imitating me or not. This seems a fairly irrelevant angle, but the fact is that I don't react very readily to any modern poetry. I was hearing a young poet give a reading of his work, and he was explaining afterwards how much he hated all the other ones his age. He was talking about one of these and I said "He has a singing line, hasn't he?" Meaning, as I thought, that he had the root of the matter in him. This chap pounced and said "That's it, you've got it! Just a writer of lyrics!" He thought that if it sounds pretty that means you're bad. Well, I thought he hadn't got the root of the matter in him. Milton could say "God damn you to hell" and make it a singing line, but these people think it's got to sound ugly or they aren't sincere. I think it's Samuel Butler who describes a wallpaper of the Victorian period, with flowers on it, and he says that some bees came in and they went to every one of the flowers all the way down and then they went to every one of the flowers all the way up and they tested every one of these right across the area, and they never realised that *none* of the flowers had any honey.

RICKS: Do you ever feel it's strange how much of your taste is really very traditional? You actually praised a bit of Swinburne at one point, didn't you?

EMPSON: Well, about Swinburne, if we're going off on to that. I think he only wrote well when—well, there are a few good things about revolutionary politics which cheered him up—but normally he only wrote well about his appalling ideas about sex, which is all about one side torturing the other. Very remote from my own ambitions in bed, but somehow it was what he wrote well about. When he is writing about that, he isn't vague, he isn't any of the things that T. S. Eliot said he was. Of course, later in life, when he became settled down, he'd got nothing to write about. He did exactly what Mr. Eliot says about him. But when he's writing well, in the first poems and ballads, he isn't any of these things at all. I think Mr. Eliot just didn't like the subject, very rightly, and said it was all about nothing, whereas it was about this slightly appalling thing. Fiddling while he burned Rome is so unlike what everyone else thinks of Nero burning Rome as being like:

When with flame all around him aspirant
Stood flushed as a harp-player stands
The implacable beautiful tyrant
Rose-crowned, having death in his hands.

The rest of the verse becomes so ludicrous that you can't read it aloud
without laughing. But that bit is what most of the Romantics had been
aiming at, finally getting into focus. I think that, though madly queer
and morally most undesirable, it is frightfully good poetry. I myself
have never been able to imitate it. But I think that most poets have been
affected by things they can't do. Coming back to my kind of poetry, I
think it's a specialised kind. I began to feel that I was beginning to
parody myself, that it was too narrow. That was why I thought it was
bad, in a way. I certainly don't think that the only good kind of poetry
is like mine: I think mine is too specialised.

RICKS: But yours is actually like lots of different things, isn't it? It
seems to me in some ways dangerous that it was first praised in terms of
Donne and the Metaphysicals, because it's obvious now that there's an
increasing dissatisfaction with Donne and the Metaphysicals.

EMPSON: I still think he's wonderful. I think he meant something: I
think he was attacking Christianity in his love poems. This has gone
completely out, it's completely out of fashion to believe that. In fact,
you're most earnestly told you mustn't. But this movement of fashion
is all nonsense: it needs to be removed. Once you realise the love poems
are defiant, you think they're good and courageous again. As long as
you think they are only fribbles by a man who fully accepted the
Church and State he was quarrelling with, you think it's in very bad
taste. Of course it seems in very bad taste if you think it's all nonsense.
So I think this misunderstanding of Donne is the result of the entirely
mistaken criticism which was led by T. S. Eliot, in a book called *A
Garland for John Donne*, which was, in fact, the kiss of death, the crown
of thorns. When I was starting writing there was a lot being written—
by Robert Graves as much as anybody—about how poetry ought to
be about a conflict: it needn't resolve a conflict (on the whole, a
Victorian opinion—"In Memoriam" was to solve the problem about
whether you live for ever or not), but he thought the poem ought to
be about a conflict which is raging in the mind of the writer but hasn't

G

been solved. He should write about the things that really worry him, in fact worry him to the point of madness. The poem is a kind of clinical object, done to prevent him from going mad. It is therefore not addressed to any public, but it is useless to him unless it is in fact clear and readable, because he has to —as it were—address it to the audience within himself. It isn't expressed unless it's a thing which somebody else can read, so if it's obscure it actually fails in this therapeutic function, it isn't saving his sanity. But nevertheless he doesn't write it for any group or—he doesn't even write it for Laura Riding. This really was the principle I was going on.

RICKS: Then why are so many of them obscure? Some of your early ones are very hard to understand, aren't they?

EMPSON: Well, all this was when I settled into it. When I started doing it, I thought it would be very nice to write beautiful things like the poet Donne. I would sit by the fire trying to think of an interesting puzzle. Although, as a matter of fact, most of them turned out to be love poems about boy being too afraid of girl to tell her anything, the simple desire to think of something rather like Donne was the basic impulse. But I think my few good ones are all on the basis of expressing an unresolved conflict. It does seem to me a very good formula which applies to a lot of kinds of poetry. I think it's completely out of fashion, isn't it? Nobody says that now. In a way, you see, as you approach middle age, though in fact you're a seething pit of scorpions, you don't recognise them in that form. You're getting things tidy: "Can I get the boy to college?" and things like that are what you are thinking about. So it doesn't appear to you in this direct way, as an unresolved conflict which you need to express in a poem. You often do feel it again when you're old, when you're seriously old, when you've been forced to retire and the pressure of making actual decisions in the world is no longer what you ought to be thinking about. The idea that you write old and young fits in with the idea of poetry as the expression of an unresolved conflict.

RICKS: But one reason why I think *The Gathering Storm* is so good is because in a way it is about practical things. It seems to me that your poems are very concerned to put what can be said for the other side:

"Courage Means Running" is, as you say, about what can be said for Munich. In this you anticipate the sort of things that A. J. P. Taylor has said about it. "Reflection from Rochester" explains how, although we hate it, we go on with the arms race.

EMPSON: Well, everybody has to think about these things, really. As a matter of fact, everybody who reads the newspapers is thinking about these things. This degree of wisdom is not at all out of the way. It isn't what poets usually write about, that's all. Most poetry today is in the Imagist tradition, and it simply isn't the fashion in poetry to understand things; people understand these things in prose perfectly well. I accept your praise with great comfort and satisfaction; I agree that the whole tendency of modern criticism has been not to encourage people to be as sensible as they would be if they had to deal with the matter really, in prose. But the more we praise the good sense of Empson, the more I feel how clever I've been, how right I was to stop writing. If I'd gone on it would have got appallingly boring. It's only because I stopped in time that you still think it's poetry.

the Review Nos. 6/7

ROBERT LOWELL IN CONVERSATION WITH A. ALVAREZ

ALVAREZ: Your verse has changed a great deal, hasn't it? Most of the mannerisms of rhythm and imagery that you used in your early poems have disappeared, and yet you now have something much more personal. Is this how you see your own work?

LOWELL: When my second book came out the most interesting review of it was by Randall Jarrell. Though he liked the book, he made the point that I was doing things I could do best quite often, and I think he quoted Kipling—when you learn how to do something, don't do it again. I think you should always do something a little longer than you should, go on until it gives out. There was a long pause between the second and the third. I didn't want to go just cranking the same machine.

ALVAREZ: When your first poems came out you were a Catholic, weren't you? You've ceased to be one since. Has the change in style anything to do with this change in allegiance?

LOWELL: It may have. In the second book I wasn't a Catholic but I was using Catholic material from a non-Catholic point of view, a neutral one. In *Life Studies* I was very anxious to get a tone that sounded a little like conversation.

ALVAREZ: I felt that in *Life Studies* you were setting your personal house in order, you were dealing with the very personal material almost as you would in psychoanalysis. It seemed that, having left behind the dogmatic Catholic base and the dogmatic rhythms and symbols that went with it, you were trying to build a new base from which you could work.

LOWELL: I had in the back of my mind something like the prose of a Chekhov short story. The poems came in two spurts. The first was more intense when two-thirds of the autobiographical poems were written. This was a period of, at most, three months. Then there was a second period which finished that group and filled in blank spaces.

ALVAREZ: I remember someone in *the Review* saying that the prose section in your book—which unfortunately wasn't published in the English version—was often more concentrated than one or two of the poems about your relatives. Do you think that's a fair comment?

LOWELL: There's a long first section in *Life Studies* called "Last Afternoon with Uncle Devereux Winslow" which was originally written in prose. I put it aside and I later cut things out and re-arranged it and made different transitions and put it into verse, so there is that connection and perhaps the style comes out of writing prose. But I'd say that the prose was an awful job to do. It took a long time and I think it could be less concentrated with more sting or something like that.

ALVAREZ: You don't find prose comes naturally?

LOWELL: I find it very hard. I like to revise and when you have something of thirty or forty pages written as carefully as a poem—and it was written that carefully—it's very hard.

ALVAREZ: Do you revise your poems much?

LOWELL: Usually. I think my record is a poem that was finished in one day. Usually it's a long time. I would have said that writing free verse you're more likely to get a few lines that are right in the beginning than you are in metre.

ALVAREZ: My own interpretation of *Life Studies* is that the family poems cleared the ground and that, with the now very famous poems like "Man and Wife", "Home After Three Months Away", and "Waking in the Blue", your own choice came up absolutely clear— they have this unmistakable Lowell rhythm.

LOWELL: They are not written chronologically. Actually the first poem finished was "Skunk Hour" and I think the second was "Man and Wife", though they were all going on at the same time. But the first nut to crack really was "Skunk Hour"—that was the hardest. I cast about . . . it was written backwards, more or less, and I added the first four stanzas after I'd finished it.

ALVAREZ: It came before these family poems?

LOWELL: Yes, actually it was the first, although the others were sort of started. I guess the first thing I had was a very imperfect version of "Man and Wife", which I dropped, and then I wrote "Skunk Hour". "Skunk Hour" was the first one completed. I was reading Elizabeth Bishop's poems very carefully at the time and imitating the loose formality of her style.

ALVAREZ: It seems to me that that poem is less successful in its opening lines. It suddenly gets down to what you're really talking about in the last part.

LOWELL: The opening's sort of cotton-nosed, it's supposed to let you sink into the poem and then it tenses up. I don't know whether it works or not. You dawdle in the first part and suddenly get caught in the poem.

ALVAREZ: Confessional verse as you write it isn't simply an outpouring, is it? It's very strict, although the rules are hard to find.

LOWELL: You're asking how a confessional poem that's a work of art differs from someone's outpourings, sensational confessions for the newspapers or confessions to one's analyst. It seems to me there is some connection. When I was doing what might be called confessional poems there was a big chunk of something to be gotten out, but a great deal of it was very tame; the whole thing wasn't any very great story, but still there were things I wanted to say. Then the thing was the joy of composition, to get some music and imagination and form into it and to know just when to stop and what sort of language to put it in—it was pure joy writing it and I think it was pure technical joy, and poems are dull if you don't have that.

ALVAREZ: What about the technique? You were saying that you have a great love for William Carlos Williams, who I would say seems to be the antithetical poet to you. Has he had any effect?

LOWELL: I always liked Williams, since I was a young man. But I don't think I've ever written anything that's very much like him. He really is utterly carried away into the object, it intoxicated him in describing it, and his way of composition's so different from mine. He was an active doctor and he wrote in snatches; he developed a way of writing in which he could get things out very quickly. I find him a very artful poet, but his art was largely cutting what he poured out. My things are much more formal, much more connected with older English poetry; there's a sort of formal personality in myself. I think anyone could tell that my free verse was written by someone who'd done a lot of formal verse. I began writing in the Thirties and the current I fell into was the southern group of poets—John Crowe Ransom and Allen Tate—and that was partly a continuation of Pound and Eliot and partly an attempt to make poetry much more formal than Eliot and Pound did: to write in metres but to make the metres look hard and make them hard to write. It was the period of the famous book *Understanding Poetry*, of analysing poems to see how they're put together; there was a great emphasis on craftsmanship. Out of that, though it came later, were poetry workshops and all that sort of thing. Well, that's in my blood very much, and about 1950 it was prevailing everywhere in America. There were poets trained that way, writing in the style, writing rather complicated, difficult, laboured poems, and it was getting very dry. You felt you had to get away from that at all costs. Yet still it's in one's blood. We're trained that way and I admire Tate and Ransom as much as ever. But in England that was the period of Auden and poetry was trying to express the times, politics, psychology, economics, the war and everything that somehow wasn't very strong with us. We had such poets and we had a lot of Auden imitators, but the strongest feeling seemed to be to get away from that and just write a poem. We talked a lot about form, craft, tragic experience and things like that.

ALVAREZ: On this question of Auden, you seem to feel apparently quite strongly about not being political.

LOWELL: Well, yes, and that's quite misleading because it now seems to me that Auden's glory is that he caught all those things with much greater power than any of the people of his group. He's made the period immortal, of waiting for the war. At that time it seemed so stifled in controversy that it wasn't possible for us. People tried it in our country.

ALVAREZ: What he got really was not the politics but the neurotic tension.

LOWELL: That's a better description. He caught the air and it was air in which events were hovering over your shoulder at every point, the second war was boiling into existence. Freud and Marx and a host of thinkers who were the most alive at that time—and still are in many ways—all do get into his poetry, and the idiom of those people waiting! I find that marvellous. I don't think this is a period of parties and politics the way the Thirties were. Here and in America that all seems to have calmed down to something we imagine is more the way life ordinarily is. I don't meet people who are violently anti-Russian very often. That doesn't seem to be the air.

ALVAREZ: They still exist though.

LOWELL: They exist, but they don't exist very much in the intellectual world. While in the Thirties everybody was taking sides on something, usually very violently—violent conversions, violent Marxist positions, violent new deal, violent anti-new deal—things couldn't be more different now. The terrible danger now is of the great impersonal bureaucratic machinery rolling over everything and flattening out humanity.

ALVAREZ: The poets over here, and I would say in the States too, with the Beats, are rather cashing in on this.

LOWELL: Well, some of the Beats are quite good, but no mass movement like that can be of much artistic importance. It was a way for people to get away from the complexities of life. You've got to remain complicatedly civilised and organised to keep your humanity under the pressures of our various governments, not go into a bohemian wildness. Quite a few people are genuinely bohemian; the real bohemia is something tremendous, of course. I think someone really good, some Hart Crane, might swoop down on all this material and take it up and make art out of it. It's useful in a way that a certain amount of ice has been broken.

ALVAREZ: Do you believe in poets ganging together in schools and groups and movements and so on?

LOWELL: Literary life is just one little wave after another: there was the Auden wave and the Dylan Thomas and the anti-Dylan Thomas, and we've had similar things. Most of the good poetry does seem to come out of these waves, though you occasionally get solitary figures who have nothing to do with them. But there are few survivors, most people are left stranded on the beach. One manner seems as bad or as good as another; it freshens the atmosphere for a moment and then seems to have faults equally as disastrous as the ones it was fighting against. But what's important, every so often something enormous opens, such as French symbolism, which will go on for fifty or sixty years, with enormous talents one after another taking it up and changing it. To a certain extent we have this in America in the generation of Pound and Eliot and Marianne Moore.

[Published by permission of *The Observer* who commissioned the interview from which these extracts are selected. Further extracts can be found in *The Observer* of July 21st, 1963.]

the Review No. 8

POEMS

Michael Fried

The Garden

In Memoriam R.P.B.

July 1959. Almost six years
Ago. Your throat sunburned, your white shirt
Dripping sweat, your entire gross
Delicate body concentrated in purpose:
To exterminate a black beetle eating a rose.
Bemused, dubious, but unforgiving,
You watching him work his legs until the death-throes
Were done. Later we sat embalmed
In the clear gin we had been drinking
All evening. I kept trying to steer
Your tired monologue back toward poetry
But, implacable, you went on talking
About Maine and what you had there—
A larger garden, more books, youth, the sea
And more besides. Later still,
Having decided that I ought to eat,
And having opened a cold can of vichysoisse,
You went out—smiling and apologetic,
Equipped with a long flashlight—into the garden
To look for parsley.

Hugo Williams

The Butcher*

The butcher carves veal for two.
The cloudy, frail slices fall over his knife.

His face is hurt by the parting sinews
And he looks up with relief, laying it on the scales

He is a rose young man with white eyelashes
Like a bullock. He always serves me now.

I think he knows about my life. How we prefer
To eat in when it's cold. How someone

With a foreign accent can only cook veal.
He writes the price on the grease-proof packet

And hands it to me courteously. His smile
Is the official seal on my marriage.

* Subsequently published in *Symptoms of Loss*. Hugo Williams. O.U.P., 1965.
Reproduced by permission of the author and publishers.

Ian Hamilton

Last Illness

Entranced, you turn again and over there
It is white also. Rectangular white lawns
For miles, white walls between them. Snow.
You close your eyes. The terrible changes.

White movements in one corner of your room.
Between your hands, the flowers of your quilt
Are stormed. Dark shadows smudge
Their faded, impossible colours
But do not settle.

You hear the ice take hold. Along the street
The yellowed drifts, cleansed by a minute's fall
Wait to be fouled again. Your final breath
Is in the air, pure white, and moving fast.

Colin Falck

Denying Me

From the Spanish of Juan Ramon Jimenez

Denying me with your hands you drew me closer.
You lay quiet, with your blue eyes rimmed in red
Like precious stones.
Where did it come from, this great dying fire,
This life of yours?
Your red mouth perfect as a wound
Burns with anger the moment it leaves mine.
I garlanded you with flowers, and you let me.
You were so weak that the moth fluttering over you
Could have silenced your arms with its wings.

Thomas Clark

My Father's Death
after Gorky

My father, like a section of enamelled piping,
Floats prone in a gloom of musks and icons.

An odor of melons about to burst open
Hangs over the garden. House moths
Glide in, drawn to the bed where thick candles
Polish my father's face—

It's a block of tallow,
The kind housemaids make. The clay eyeballs
Of his toes watch from their perches;
His cheeks bulge like ripe limes.

Father, you never smiled so much before.
Now your lips lock around the silver
Heads of your eyeteeth,
That glint like carpenter's nails.
Your eyes, clear pools where my first lie
Plinked, a pebble in a glass bowl,
Are corked with copper disks.
The plugs glow like dusty suns.

Even your sockets
Hoard good Russian coins!

My mother kneels over your long body.
A brine of new sweat and kitchen soap shines
On the veins of her wrists
That distend and go slack. She is combing
Black hives of ticks out of your hair.

The comb's got teeth like German nails—
I used it as a hacksaw, to split the rinds
Of watermelons, and scrape away
Clots of seeds that ribbed the inside walls.
Like strings of shiny woodlice.

That was last summer.
You grinned. The hulls
Of your teeth glittered and cracked
With light, like white glass.

Michael Fried

Your Name

That passionate monosyllable, your name,
Like some wounded animal's mostly inarticulate
Cry, when the familiar hurt returns, on dragging legs,
After an interlude of sleep or natural anasthesia,
Spoken over and over by my own lips, wakes me.

The Answer

Loving as I do the nauseous moment
Before the green wave destroys itself,
When it is held upright only by my
Imploring glance through to its brown viscera,

How could I fail to answer
The same annihilating clarity in you,
Once having glimpsed behind your green iris
Something brown and vast heaving over.

A. Alvarez

Spring Fever

Too young to know
And far too young to care
What shapes hover
At the head of the stair

You twist your hands,
Your hair falls round your face
Darkly. The fire breeds shadows.
I keep my place

Although the rain wakes
And the blackbirds call
Fluently, fluently
The leaves uncurl

On wet apple trees.
You stretch your arms
Pleased with your body's
Fluent warmth.
But your eyes stay down.

Be wakeful. Be gentle.
Look, the dark gathers
Inside your head.
It tangles your fingers.
Your wrists fill with blood.

Be gentle. Be wakeful.
From the fire to the shadows
At the top of the stairs
Come to bed.

John Fuller

Manzu*

A girl is seated, nude and placid, lost
In quietness. The pig-tail thick and full
On flashlit shoulder blades. The ankles crossed.
Apotheosis of the animal.

This virginal formality.
A poised ragazza on a rush-seat chair,
Finds cloistral echoes. From a trinket tree
Chickens and saints puncture the thumbed-out air.

And dolphins on the slow cathedral doors
Plunge like a drowning scalp. Within their globe,
Bemitred dancers tip-toe and then pause.
The cardinal is sensual in his robe:

One sees beneath embroidery bare toes
As long as fingers. Youthful age imparts
That faintly turnip shadow to his nose,
That silent smile, affinity of parts.

The buds are breaking. No one is annoyed.
It is a simple drama. Lavish, yes,
But white and delicate. And eyes avoid
The bland Italian ritual of flesh.

* Subsequently published in *The Tree That Walked*. John Fuller. Chatto &
Windus, 1966. Reproduced by permission of the author and publishers.